THEIR FIRST TIME
IN THE MOVIES

LES KRANTZ

THE OVERLOOK PRESS
WOODSTOCK NEW YORK

For Margie

ACKNOWLEDGMENTS

Many heads, hands, and hearts were lent to this book. I am especially grateful to Peter Mayer, my collaborator and the publisher of Overlook, who provided wisdom and good judgment. And to Tim Knight, my manuscript editor, whose encyclopedic knowledge and literary sensibilities were assets beyond measure, and Tracy Carns, Publishing Director of Overlook, whose hands-on attention and expertise were invaluable. Without the foregoing three individuals, this book would not be the same.

My thanks to my wife Margie, who put up with my stargazing vigil during every holiday and weekend for almost a year; Various folks at The Overlook Press, including George Davidson, David Chestnut, David Mulrooney, Hermann Lademann, Stephen Cipriano, Maureen Nagy, Jane Lahr, Olga Sala, and Susanne Guttermuth. Susan Bowles, Bob Thaller, Bryan Rowles, Ariel Herrera, Paola Cornacchia, Nathan Buck, Elias Savada, Marc Berlin, Glen Brodie, Ron Harvey, Howard Mandelbaum, Ron Mandelbaum, Bill Berrios, Marvin Tiano, Jack Tiano, Larry Edmunds, Dustin Hoffman, Anne Bancroft, Toni Howard, Jill L. Smith, Stacy Tolbart, Steve Sellers, Murray Glass, Roger Memos, Dick Krantz, Tim Lanza, Jeff Joseph, Anne Lewis, Roni Lubliner, Conrad Sprout, Renee Kibbler, Arlene Goldberg, Tilman Reitzle, Michael Yakaitis, John Kirchner, and Dane Ronvik.

CONTRIBUTING WRITERS: Sue Sveum, Andy Coan, Bob Kalish, Joe Dungan
CONTRIBUTING EDITOR: Frank Scatoni
MANUSCRIPT EDITOR: Tim Knight
COPY EDITOR: Janis Hunt
RESEARCH: Matt Blankman, Nick Boecher, Yolanda Buggs, Veronika Finkova, Mike Marcoe, Joyce Rock, Kristin Todd
EDITORIAL ASSISTANCE: Carol Stangby
INTERIOR DESIGN: Fabia Wargin
DOCUMENTARY PRODUCER: George Elder
DOCUMENTARY EDITOR: Scott Dummler
DOCUMENTARY NARRATOR: Pete Stacker

First published in the United States in 2001 by
The Overlook Press, Peter Mayer Publishers, Inc.
Woodstock and New York
WOODSTOCK: One Overlook Drive, Woodstock, NY 12498
(for individual orders, bulk and special sales, contact our Woodstock office)
NEW YORK: 141 Wooster Street, New York, NY 10012
www.overlookpress.com

Copyright © 2001 FTM Books, Inc.

Library of Congress Cataloging-in-Publication Data
Krantz, Les.
Their first time : in the movies / Les Krantz.
p. cm.
ISBN 1-58567-198-3
1. Motion picture actors and actresses—United States—Biography. I. Title.
PN1998.5 .K73 2001
791.43'028'092—dc21
[B]   2001036558

Manufactured in Hong Kong
FIRST EDITION
1 3 5 7 9 8 6 4 2

ISBN 1-58567-198-3

PHOTO CREDITS

Left to Right and Top to Bottom
The photographs on the following pages were provided courtesy of:

Page 1: Everett Collection; Photofest; Photofest. 2: Photofest; Photofest; Les Krantz Collection. 3: Les Krantz Collection; Photofest; Les Krantz Collection. 4: Everett Collection; Larry Edmunds Book Store. 5: Photofest. 6: Everett Collection; Everett Collection. 7: Everett Collection. 8: Photofest; Everett Collection; Photofest; Photofest. 9: Everett Collection; Photofest; Photofest; Photofest. 10: Photofest; Photofest; Photofest. 11: Les Krantz Collection; Photofest; Photofest. 12: Photofest; Les Krantz Collection. 13: Everett Collection. 14: Photofest. 15: Photofest; Larry Edmunds Book Store. 16: Photofest; Larry Edmunds Book Store. 17: Larry Edmunds Book Store. 18: Photofest; Photofest; Photofest; Photofest. 19: Photofest; Photofest. 20: Photofest; Photofest; Photofest. 21: Photofest. 22: Everett Collection; Larry Edmunds Book Store; Photofest. 23: Photofest. 24: Photofest; Larry Edmunds Book Store. 25: Everett Collection. 26: Photofest. 27: Photofest; Photofest. 28: Everett Collection; Photofest. 29: Everett Collection. 30: Everett Collection; Larry Edmunds Book Store. 31: Everett Collection; Everett Collection. 32: Everett Collection. 33: Photofest; Photofest. 34: Photofest; Photofest. 35: Everett Collection. 36: Photofest; Photofest. 37: Photofest. 38: Everett Collection. 39: Photofest; Larry Edmunds Book Store; Photofest. 40: Photofest; Larry Edmunds Book Store. 41: Photofest. 42: Photofest; Photofest. 43: Everett Collection. 44: Everett Collection. 45: Photofest; Everett Collection; Larry Edmunds Book Store. 46: Photofest. 47: Everett Collection; Photofest. 48: Everett Collection; Everett Collection. 49: Everett Collection. 50: Everett Collection. 51: Photofest; Photofest. 52: Everett Collection; Larry Edmunds Book Store; Everett Collection. 53: Photofest. 54: Photofest; Photofest; Photofest; Everett Collection. 55: Photofest; Everett Collection; Photofest; Les Krantz Collection; Photofest. 56: Photofest: Photofest; Photofest. 57: Everett Collection; Photofest; Everett Collection. 58: Les Krantz Collection; Everett Collection; Photofest. 59: Photofest; Everett Collection; Photofest. 60: Photofest; Photofest. 61: Everett Collection. 62: Everett Collection. 63: Photofest; Photofest. 64: Les Krantz Collection; Photofest. 65: Les Krantz Collection. 66: Photofest. 67: Everett Collection; Photofest. 68: Photofest; Photofest. 69: Photofest. 70: Photofest; Larry Edmunds Book Store; Photofest. 71: Photofest; Photofest. 72: Larry Edmunds Book Store. 73: Photofest; Photofest; Photofest. 74: Photofest. 75: Photofest; Les Krantz Collection; Everett Collection. 76: Photofest. 77: Photofest; Photofest. 78: Everett Collection; Larry Edmunds Book Store. 79: Photofest. 80: Everett Collection. 81: Everett Collection; Photofest. 82: Photofest; Photofest. 83: Everett Collection. 84: Photofest; Photofest. 85: Everett Collection. 86: Everett Collection. 87: Photofest; Photofest. 88: Photofest; Photofest. 89: Photofest. 90: Photofest. 91: Les Krantz Collection; Photofest. 92: Larry Edmunds Book Store; Photofest. 93: Photofest. 94: Photofest. 95: Everett Collection; Photofest. 96: Photofest. 97: Photofest. 98: Everett Collection. 99: Photofest; Everett Collection. 100: Everett Collection; Photofest; Larry Edmunds Book Store. 101: Everett Collection. 102: Photofest. 103: Photofest; Les Krantz Collection. 104: Everett Collection. 105: Everett Collection; Photofest. 106: Photofest; Les Krantz Collection. 107: Photofest. 108: Photofest. 109: Photofest; Everett Collection. 110: Photofest; Photofest. 111: Photofest. 112: Everett Collection. 113: Photofest; Photofest. 114: Photofest; Photofest; Photofest; Photofest; Photofest. 115: Photofest; Photofest; Photofest. 116: Photofest; Photofest; Photofest. 117: Photofest; Photofest; Photofest. 118: Photofest; Les Krantz Collection. 119: Photofest; Photofest; Photofest. 120: Les Krantz Collection; Photofest. 121: Photofest. 122: Photofest. 123: Les Krantz Collection; Photofest. 124: Photofest; Photofest. 125: Everett Collection. 126: Photofest. 127: Photofest; Les Krantz Collection. 128: Photofest; Photofest. 129: Photofest. 130: Photofest. 131: Photofest; Photofest. 132: Everett Collection; Everett Collection. 133: Everett Collection. 134: Photofest. 135: Photofest; Everett Collection. 136: Photofest; Photofest. 137: Photofest. 138: Photofest. 139: Photofest; Photofest. 140: Photofest; Les Krantz Collection. 141: Photofest. 142: Photofest. 143: Photofest; Photofest. 144: Photofest; Everett Collection. 145: Photofest; Photofest. 146: Everett Collection. 147: Photofest; Photofest. 148: Photofest; Photofest. 149: Les Krantz Collection. 150: Photofest; Photofest; Photofest; Photofest; Photofest. 151: Photofest; Photofest; Photofest. 152: Photofest; Photofest; Photofest; Photofest. 153: Photofest; Photofest; Photofest.

CONTENTS

THE ESSENCE OF IT

In the late twenties, eccentric British novelist Elinor Glyn defined stardom as having "it." *Their First Time in the Movies* is about what "it" is.

There are no statistics that I am familiar with that quantify the success rate of aspiring actors who go to Hollywood; yet every actor that has succeeded has had their share of obstacles to overcome, and often began in roles far less glamorous than they had envisioned.

Gary Cooper started as a stuntman; Marilyn Monroe's first movie credit was for the role of a waitress who only briefly appeared onscreen; John Travolta debuted as a teenage zombie possessed by the devil. On the other hand, Kirk Douglas started as Barbara Stanwyck's costar; Kim Novak's acting debut was a starring part opposite Fred MacMurray; and Meryl Streep earned her first movie role playing opposite Jane Fonda.

Regardless of the details of their first strides out of the gate, the quest of hopeful actors may be the ultimate against-the-odds adventure. Unlike the plots of the many movies about beating the odds—*A Star is Born, Funny Girl,* and *Rocky,* to name a few—the ascent is often about more than just sheer determination. Frequently, a budding career is fostered by less intrinsic forces. Humphrey Bogart and Jack Lemmon were from wealthy families; Burt Reynolds was a football star; and Julia Roberts's career was nurtured by her show-business family. The diversity tells us something: the moment the camera rolls, only one thing counts—the ability to convincingly portray a character. It's called *acting.*

But there are many great actors, some who earn little money or recognition. Why do others become cultural icons with international followings? In reading this book and viewing the accompanying documentary, you will reach your own conclusion about what "it" is. Every actor discussed has "it", regardless of how foolish or inexperienced they may have looked on their first try—and some indeed did make fools of themselves, as you'll see. Others, even that first time out, looked as good as the stars they eventually became. The fact that such opposites exist in the seeds of stardom is perhaps the most amazing and entertaining aspect of my book. I give it to you as my effort to capture the essence of "it"… and hopefully to captivate your imagination, too. It is, after all, imagination that provides a glimpse of what could be—and the pages that follow are about people like you and me who liked what they imagined enough to *act* on it.

— *Les Krantz*

Before he was a star, Gary Cooper was a stunt man in silent films of the mid-1920s.

Julia Roberts opposite Richard Gere in her Oscar-nominated performance in Pretty Woman *(1990), a movie that catapulted her to stardom, less than two years after she debuted in a low-budget teen comedy.*

(facing page) Marilyn Monroe started as a face in the crowd in a low budget flop, Dangerous Years *(1947).*

1900-1919

The scene that scandalized the nation —The kiss from The Widow Jones (1896) — one of the first motion pictures developed by Thomas Edison.

George Barnes in The Great Train Robbery (1903).

Mary Pickford's debut in 1908. She eventually became known as "America's Sweetheart."

THE BIRTH OF THE STAR MACHINE

Moving pictures created quite a stir with the public when they first began to appear at the turn of the century. The close-up of a kiss in Edison Studios' short, *The Widow Jones,* scandalized viewers, who were still in the iron grip of strict Victorian morality. Brushing aside the controversy, Edison continued to produce one-reel films. His company was one of three wooing the public to shell out their pennies at "peep shows." Had early filmmakers continued making these crude, rudimentary one-reelers, audiences would have soon tired of them, confirming naysayers' predictions that the moving picture was nothing more than a fad. But a handful of filmmakers saw the inherent storytelling possibilities in the new medium and began developing a more complex film language. In 1902, a French magician turned director, Georges Méliés, unveiled the prototypical science fiction adventure, *A Trip to the Moon,* based on the Jules Verne story. In America, pioneer filmmaker Edwin S. Porter thrilled audiences with his landmark western, *The Great Train Robbery* (1903). Shot on location in New Jersey, Porter's one-reel, ten-minute fictional film marked several firsts in American cinema: it was the first motion picture to tell a story, the first shot non-sequentially and edited to fit the storyline, and the first western. It also was the first smash hit.

The success of *The Great Train Robbery* led to the building of the first permanent movie theaters in the United States. These Nickelodeons (so named because of the nickel admission fee) sprang up across the country. By 1910, moving pictures were regularly playing at Nickelodeons or in vaudeville theaters as part of the entertainment schedule.

Despite their growing popularity with audiences, motion pictures were still regarded by most critics as cheap, lowbrow entertainment. Most serious actors shunned the new medium, preferring the stage to the screen. Appearing in a motion picture seemed like a lose/lose situation; it could potentially undermine, rather than enhance, an actor's reputation in the theater. Also, cost-conscious film producers refused to credit the actors, fearing that they would demand more money if the public knew them by name. There were no stars, only anonymous, interchangeable players.

This critical antipathy towards movies began to erode in 1912, the year French director Louis Mercanton premiered his opulent costume drama, *Queen Elizabeth,* starring the legendary stage actress Sarah Bernhardt. Hailed as the greatest actress of the era, Bernhardt gave the medium a much-needed shot of respectability. That same year, producer Carl Laemmle placed an ad in a popular magazine refuting the news story that actress Florence Lawrence, previously known only as "The Biograph Girl," had been killed in a streetcar accident. Laemmle then sent Lawrence on a nationwide publicity tour, where she was mobbed by adoring fans. As Laemmle suspected, Florence Lawrence had become the attraction, not the motion picture itself. The star system was born.

Motion pictures were becoming more and more sophisticated. As running times expanded beyond one film reel in length, one of the industry's greatest pioneers was experimenting with such early techniques as cross-cutting, close-ups, establishing shots, and camera movement. D.W. Griffith did much to advance the development of cinematic storytelling in the second decade of the twentieth century.

The son of a doctor impoverished by the Civil War, Griffith was born in Kentucky in 1875. He went to work for the Biograph Company in 1908 as an actor and screenwriter, for a salary of five dollars a day to act and fifteen dollars for any ideas contributed to the film. In time he became the head of production at Biograph. His first year on the job, Griffith directed over 100 films. In the end, he directed nearly 450 films for Biograph before leaving to supervise production for the Mutual Film Corporation. Ambitious to use his technical skills on an important film, he began to look for an epic to adapt. He chose *The Clansman,* a Civil War-era novel written by the Reverend Thomas Dixon. Starring Henry B. Walthall, Lillian Gish, and Mae Marsh, *The Birth of a Nation,* as the movie was titled, eventually cost more than $90,000. With battle scenes featuring hundreds of extras, it astonished filmgoers. President Woodrow Wilson referred to the film as "like history written with lightning."

Not one to rest on his laurels, Griffith tackled an even broader historical canvas with his next film, *Intolerance.* To depict man's inhumanity to man through the ages, Griffith recreated the fall of ancient Babylon, the crucifixion of Christ, the St. Bartholomew's Day massacre of the Huguenots in France, and a modern story of labor unrest. At a cost of $2.5 million, *Intolerance* was truly a mammoth undertaking. The Babylonian sequence alone featured over four thousand extras. Despite critical praise, it was a resounding flop with audiences, who were both confused and bored by Griffith's complex treatment of his theme.

Inspired by Griffith's achievements, other directors began pushing the boundaries of the medium. Mack Sennett, a former student of Griffith, left the master to establish a comic dynasty at Keystone Studios. Under his guidance, such stars as Fatty Arbuckle, Mabel Normand, and Ben Turpin honed and refined their talents for slapstick comedy. Cecil B. DeMille embarked on his long career as a populist director, making both westerns and marital farces starring Gloria Swanson. Director Thomas Ince also gained renown for his westerns during this time, though he is more remembered today for dying mysteriously aboard William Randolph Hearst's yacht than for any of his films.

By the time America entered World War I, the motion picture industry was in full flower and growing under pressure from an entertainment-needy audience. But by the end of the war there had been a shake-out of motion picture companies. Biograph folded, but the seeds for major studios like Paramount, MGM, Fox, and Universal were all planted during this time. With the growth of studios, the actors became even more of a commodity — perhaps none more so than Mary Pickford.

Known for her winning smile and angelic curls, Mary Pickford was christened "America's Sweetheart" in 1913. A shrewd businesswoman, Pickford soon became the highest paid movie star of the era, commanding upwards of ten thousand dollars a week. Her male counterpart at the box office was the English music hall actor, Charlie Chaplin. A gifted comedian, he came to America and soon found steady work as one of Mack Sennett's Keystone Kops. Real success was assured when he debuted his "Little Tramp" character in a Sennett short in 1914. By the end of the decade, Chaplin was making as much money as Pickford and joined her, Douglas Fairbanks, and D.W. Griffith in launching their own film studio, United Artists.

By 1920, the studios were churning out over 600 movies a year, a rate of just under twelve per week. Florence Lawrence was already forgotten, her place taken by such stars as Tom Mix, Theda Bara, William S. Hart, Pearl White, Francis X. Bushman, and Rin Tin Tin, to name a few. Nickelodeons were gone, replaced by ornate movie theaters known as "dream palaces." By 1916, there were more than twenty-one thousand such theaters in the country, some seating more than 3,000 people. The movies had fully arrived.

In 1913 a former street urchin comes to Hollywood from London — Charlie Chaplin.

The Birth of a Nation (1915) proved how emotionally powerful a movie could be. It used the first "sound system," in which simulated dialogue, music and sound effects were performed by a live crew behind the movie screen.

America's first matinee idol — Rudolph Valentino makes his debut in 1917.

CHARLIE CHAPLIN

Charles Chaplin, circa 1916, signing a contract with the Mutual Film Corporation.

In 1921, after starring in numerous shorts, Chaplin starred in his first feature-length film, The Kid (with Jackie Coogan).

The evolution of cinema from flickering novelty to art form is due in no small part to the work of Charlie Chaplin, the preeminent genius of the silent screen. Best known for his signature role as "The Little Tramp," Chaplin took the crude slapstick of Mack Sennett and gave it an emotional depth and resonance that is never maudlin. Often hapless but never defeated, The Little Tramp rebounds from disaster with a sunny resilience that endeared him to early movie audiences, who saw him as a comic everyman of acrobatic skill and precise timing. Of course, it took Chaplin endless retakes to achieve that illusion of effortless grace under pressure. A tireless perfectionist, he reportedly agonized over every gag and every aside, twisting and tweaking the elements until the scene played to his liking. The true art of Chaplin was surely that the comedy never looks forced or studied, but utterly natural and spontaneous.

The dapper comedian behind The Little Tramp was born Charles Spencer Chaplin on April 16, 1889, into a family of London music hall entertainers. His career began at age five, when he stepped in to perform for his ailing mother. Three years later he joined a touring musical show called *The Eight Lancaster Lads,* and he continued to perform small roles in touring shows for much of his childhood.

The life of traveling stage players was difficult and often left the Chaplin family in dire economic straits. The tenuousness of family life was further strained when Chaplin's father died of acute alcoholism; grief-stricken, Chaplin's mother suffered a breakdown and was confined to an asylum. Left to fend for themselves, Chaplin and his older brother found temporary shelter in workhouses and orphanages and worked a variety of miserable jobs for little money. It was a grim existence for a child, but Chaplin never surrendered to it and focused his energies on returning to the stage.

Escape arrived when Chaplin landed a place in the Karno Comedy Troupe, a musical troupe, which regularly toured America's vaudeville circuit. At the end of one tour, Chaplin returned to the troupe's Philadelphia office to find an unsigned telegram from famed Keystone Kops producer Mack Sennett. Chaplin was initially confused by the telegram, which instructed him to contact Sennett's lawyer. He decided that it was probably nothing more than a notice about collecting his inheritance from a relative.

As it turned out, Sennett's Keystone Studios had just lost its leading comedian and needed some fresh talent. When he finally arranged a meeting with Chaplin, Sennett offered him a contract for twice what he was making with Karno. Testing his luck, Chaplin pressed for a full-year deal at a slightly higher salary; Sennett agreed — one of the great comedy partnerships in film history was born.

Before he could start with Keystone, Chaplin had to satisfy his obligations to Karno — six more months of touring. He moved to Hollywood in December of 1913 after the tour was completed and started right to work. As a somewhat reserved Englishman, Chaplin felt out of place on the rowdy Keystone set, where physical gags extended into off-camera life and roughhousing was commonplace. But eventually he established his own identity in the frantic life of the studio.

In these early days of cinema, most of Keystone's movies were unscripted shorts, thrown together as they were shot. Chaplin's first role came in just such a film, titled *Making a Living* (1914). He plays an English swindler who repeatedly matches wits with a newspaper reporter, going after the reporter's wallet, girlfriend, and finally his job. In a monocle, top hat, and walrus mustache, Chaplin plays his role with customary verve, but his sure comic touch is painfully lacking from the short, which — in Keystone fashion — consists of frenetic chase scenes punctuated by fistfights.

Making the short had been a frustrating experience for Chaplin, who didn't like how he looked onscreen and then watched director Henry Lehrman cut many of his original gags. Later that year he threw aside the monocle, top hat, and walrus mustache to introduce The Little Tramp in *Kid Auto Races At Venice*. The downtrodden hero of working class audiences, and one of the great iconic images of the century, was born.

The preeminent genius of the silent screen ... Chaplin's cinematic legacy endures.

MARY PICKFORD

"Little Mary,"
the first character
Pickford portrayed in films, was an
adaptation of the "Baby Gladys" she
portrayed on stage until 1908, the year
she began making movies.

When she was twenty-seven, Pickford
played a girl of twelve in Pollyanna
(1920).

Although Charlie Chaplin is now regarded by many as the greatest artist of the silent screen, it was Mary Pickford who was the first movie star. Her golden curls, and her vaunted purity were instantly recognizable from coast to coast and around the globe. And with the same artistry and fierce determination that made her the screen's first superstar, in 1916 she commanded a star's salary — upwards of $10,000 a week!

Pickford became a star playing child heroines who overcome adversity through their innocence and pluck. To the amazement of audiences and critics alike, Pickford convincingly played children and adolescents well into her thirties. She wore flats, bound her breasts and refused all but the chastest of screen kisses in order to perpetuate her image as the ageless heroine with the mantle of golden curls.

Pickford's early years read like one of her film's scenarios at its most melodramatic. The eldest of three in a family of actors, she was born Gladys Marie Smith on April 8, 1893, in Toronto. As a result of her father's chronic alcoholism, the Smith family lived like paupers. His death only exacerbated the family's poverty; at one point, Pickford's mother seriously entertained the family doctor's offer to adopt Gladys and thereby lessen the family's financial burden. Yet the bond between daughter and mother was ultimately too intense for them to separate, and the doctor's offer was declined. Their dire circumstances only strengthened the young girl's resolve to become the family's financial savior. She was constantly on stage, often touring for weeks at a time. Save for fellow child actors Lillian and Dorothy Gish, she didn't form any lasting friendships during her years on the road. Her mother became her manager, protector, and closest confidante.

Even as a teenager, Mary Pickford impressed many as both a gifted actress and steely negotiator. Her charm, work ethic, and frank ambition won over Broadway impresario David Belasco, who hired her to star in the play *The Warrens of Virginia* in 1907. Belasco also persuaded her to choose a stage name more appropriate for an ingénue than Gladys Smith, which sounded neither glamorous nor youthful. After much deliberation, they settled on the old family name of Pickford and changed her middle name of Marie to Mary — Mary Pickford was born.

In the early years of the twentieth century, Broadway was regarded as the zenith for serious actors. Only the most desperate or shortsighted actor would consider appearing in the flickering two-reelers playing at the nickelodeons. This concern didn't deter Pickford, however, who had just finished a theatrical run and was looking to pick up extra money during the summer months. Well aware of the antipathy towards the new medium, she swallowed her reservations and went to American Biograph studios to meet with a neophyte director named D.W. Griffith.

After watching her play a scene with actor Owen Moore, Griffith offered Pickford $5 a day on an as-needed basis. Pickford countered with a demand of $25 a week and jobs for her siblings Jack and Lottie — a startling request from a 16-year-old girl acting as her own agent. In an era when girls were expected to be coy and never discuss anything as vulgar as money, Pickford was direct and remarkably savvy in business. She got her money and joined Griffith's stock company.

Pickford's earliest film, *Mrs. Jones Entertains* (1908), has a "Dorothy Nicholson" in the cast, which was a pseudonym she chose, perhaps thinking that being in such lowbrow entertainment would be harmful to her budding stage career. Florence Lawrence, who

would soon achieve fame as "The Biograph Girl," plays the title role. The 11-minute short also features Mack Sennett.

The first "Mary Pickford" film, *The Violin Maker of Cremona* (1908), is a romantic melodrama. She plays a demure village beauty whose hand in marriage is to be given to whoever can make the finest violin. Happily, true love prevails and Pickford and her suitor embrace before a cheering crowd.

A shrewd businesswoman who went on to co-found United Artists, Pickford eventually tired of playing youngsters who champion the rights of the downtrodden, and attempted to broaden her image with more sophisticated roles. These films were received coolly by Pickford's adoring fans, however, who wanted her to remain forever "America's Sweetheart."

She wore flats, bound her breasts and refused all but the chastest of screen kisses to perpetuate her image as the ageless heroine with the mantle of golden curls.

SILENT SIRENS

Long before *The Jazz Singer* ushered in the era of the talkies in 1927, there were actresses who "spoke" to audiences through their eloquent facial expressions and body language. Running the gamut from vamp to virtuous heroine, these charismatic actresses live on in the flickering shadows of silent cinema.

Lillian Gish started her acting career on the stage when she was five. Lillian's mother and sister Dorothy were also actresses; the three made their screen debuts in D.W. Griffith's film, *An Unseen Enemy*, in 1912. As a member of Griffith's repertory company, Gish became a star following her performance in *The Birth of a Nation* (1915). A delicate, waif-like heroine, Gish made several more films with Griffith, including the classics *Broken Blossoms* (1919) and *Way Down East* (1920). Known as "The First Lady of the Silent Screen," Gish received a special Oscar to honor her film career in 1970.

Gloria Swanson, the daughter of an Army officer, attended schools in more than a dozen cities before settling in Chicago as a teenager. She met and soon married character actor Wallace Beery in 1916. The couple soon moved to Hollywood where Swanson appeared in almost twenty shorts within a two-year span. Her first feature film, *Society for Sale* (1918), was a success. Swanson soon became one of the undisputed queens of the silent screen, known as much for her style as for her acting ability in such risqué marital farces as Cecil B. DeMille's *Don't Change Your Husband* and *Male and Female* (both 1919).

Lillian Gish (top), Gloria Swanson (bottom)

SILENT COWBOYS

Ever since *The Great Train Robbery* (1903), movies about cowboys and the Wild West have been one of Hollywood's most enduring crowd-pleasing genres. Over the years, however, the western has evolved into a complex meditation on the nature of violence and morality, thanks to the films of John Ford, Sergio Leone, and Sam Peckinpah. The following silent stars set the model for later screen cowboys like John Wayne, Gene Autry, Roy Rogers, and Clint Eastwood.

William S. Hart

William S. Hart was an acclaimed Shakespearean actor on Broadway before he moved to the silver screen. In fact, he was 49 years old before he appeared in his first film, as an abusive husband in a 1914 western melodrama, *His Hour of Manhood*. Reportedly unhappy with this film, Hart became a star in *The Bargain* (1915), where he plays a stage robber redeemed by the love of a good woman. A student of the Wild West, Hart later directed and starred in a series of westerns that won critical praise for their stark realism.

Tom Mix, the son of a lumberman, was perhaps the hardest working cowboy in the business. In the span of six years, Mix appeared in more than a hundred shorts, mostly as a wrangler. Mix had started his career in a rodeo show, where he was considered one of the best riders around. In 1909, he transferred his cowboy skills to the big screen, debuting in *The Cowboy Millionaire*. Working with producer William Fox, Mix later became the biggest cowboy star of the silent era with their first collaboration, *Hearts and Saddles* (1917). More than just an actor, Mix also produced and directed several westerns, leaving his mark on the genre that made him famous.

Tom Mix

OTHER STARS OF THE PERIOD

Douglas Fairbanks   W.C. Fields   Buster Keaton   Harold Lloyd

Lon Chaney was born to deaf-mute parents and as a result learned to communicate through facial expression and pantomime. He was attracted to theater as a youth and, in 1912, struck out for Hollywood, where he earned the nickname "Man of a Thousand Faces" both for his expertise in the art of make-up and his ability to play a wide variety of parts. His first film role was in 1913, in *Poor Jake's Demise*, but his breakthrough role came in *The Miracle Man* (1919), in which he plays a crook masquerading as a cripple. Drawn to the macabre, Chaney would become a star following his performance as the deformed bell ringer Quasimodo in *The Hunchback of Notre Dame* (1923).

Douglas Fairbanks is generally acknowledged as the screen's first swashbuckler, the gloriously acrobatic star of such films as *The Mark of Zorro* (1920) and *The Black Pirate* (1926). Already established as a talented stage actor, Fairbanks left Broadway for Hollywood in 1915. He made his screen debut that year in *The Lamb*, a comic adventure that gave Fairbanks ample opportunity to demonstrate his physical bravado and cheeky humor. His stardom continued to increase, and in 1919 he co-founded United Artists with his wife Mary Pickford, Charlie Chaplin, and D.W. Griffith.

W.C. Fields, born William Claude Dukenfield, left home at the age of eleven to become a juggler. This unique talent led to a career on the vaudeville circuit, where he began developing his signature comic persona as an unrepentant misanthrope. After several well-received international stage performances, Fields appeared in his first two films, *Pool Sharks* and *His Lordship's Dilemma*, in 1915. It would be another nine years before Fields appeared in his next film, but by then his stardom had already been established. Fields starred in several shorts and feature films, and with the advent of talkies he positioned himself as one of the greatest comedic actors of all time.

Buster Keaton entered show business as a toddler. His mother and father were long-time road-show performers who incorporated three-year-old Keaton into the act as an acrobat and comedian. After the family show broke up years later, Keaton decided to try his hand at film. In 1917, he was cast in *The Butcher Boy*, the first in a series of shorts starring Fatty Arbuckle. A poker-faced clown who nimbly skirts disaster, Keaton would come into his own as a filmmaker in the twenties with such films as *Sherlock Jr.* (1924) and *The General* (1927).

Harold Lloyd began his movie career in 1912 as an extra, appearing as a scantily dressed Indian. He went on to bit parts in several Keystone comedies and finally made a name for himself as Lonesome Luke, a character he patterned after Charlie Chaplin's Little Tramp. From 1916 to 1917, he made over 100 Lonesome Luke shorts. Called "The King of Daredevil Comedy" for his athleticism and gravity-defying stunt work, Lloyd played a hapless everyman thrust into extraordinary circumstances. *A Sailor-Made Man* (1921) is Lloyd's first feature-length film.

1920-1929

George O'Brien and
Madge Bellamy in
The Iron Horse
(1924).

Mary Philbin and
Lon Chaney in
The Phantom of the
Opera (1925).

The incomparable Ben-Hur *(1925).*

THE RISE OF THE DREAM FACTORY

Motion pictures became an integral part of the cultural landscape in the 1920s. The public looked to Hollywood as "the dream factory," a perception that continues to this day. Buoyed by the post-war prosperity and the public's growing fascination with movie stars, men like Louis B. Mayer, Adolph Zucker, and the brothers Warner plucked many actors from obscurity to coddle or bully to stardom.

Box office favorites Mary Pickford, Douglas Fairbanks, and Charlie Chaplin ran their own studio, United Artists, along with partner D.W. Griffith. Offscreen, Pickford found her match — and mate — in Fairbanks, a charming swashbuckler known for his often gravity-defying stunt work in such films as *The Mark of Zorro* (1920) and *The Thief of Bagdad* (1924).

Like Pickford, Chaplin created a persona that has become film legend: "The Little Tramp" is a tender-hearted, often wily figure who usually skirts the edge of comic disaster in such films as *The Kid* (1921) and *The Gold Rush* (1925). His contemporaries, Buster Keaton and Harold Lloyd, also continued raising the bar of silent screen comedy — often at great physical risk — in such films as *The General* (1927) and *Safety Last* (1923).

When audiences weren't gasping at Chaplin's or Keaton's acrobatics, they found eye-popping spectacle in such epics as Cecil B. DeMille's *The Ten Commandments* (1923) and *King of Kings* (1927). Studio craftsmen transformed backlots into exotic locales. Nowhere is this more apparent than in *Ben-Hur* (1925). This biblical epic was plagued by production problems: directors were fired, actors replaced, and plans to film in Italy scrapped, forcing the entire production to relocate to Hollywood. Despite having all the earmarks of a critical and financial disaster, *Ben-Hur* was a smash success, with audiences thrilling to the chariot race sequence.

Audiences also flocked to westerns featuring such stars as William S. Hart and Tom Mix. Directors James Cruze and John Ford took their productions on location, and freed from the constraints of the studio, Cruze's *The Covered Wagon* (1923) and Ford's *The Iron Horse* (1924) impressed audiences and critics alike with their authenticity.

The horror film also came of age artistically during the twenties and Hollywood began making elaborate gothic horror films, many starring Lon Chaney, "The Man of a Thousand Faces." A true chameleon, Chaney painfully contorted and twisted his features to become the title character in *The Phantom of the Opera* (1925).

The freewheeling Jazz Age inspired filmmakers to depict the newfound freedom in music, fashion, and values. Women bobbed their hair, raised their hemlines, and danced the Charleston. The flapper, immortalized by such stars as Colleen Moore, Clara Bow, and Louise Brooks, had a refreshing sexual abandon. Sweden's Greta Garbo further changed the onscreen image of female sexuality. Her passionate, erotic love scenes opposite John Gilbert in *Flesh and the Devil* (1926) electrified audiences, who had never seen anyone quite like her in American films.

Another European émigré to Hollywood, Rudolph Valentino, made an immediate sensation dancing the tango in *The Four Horsemen of the Apocalypse* (1921). With his smoldering, exotic good looks and seductive gaze, Valentino won legions of devoted female admirers with his performance in *The Sheik* (1921).

His sudden death at age 31 ensured his mythic status in film history, but one can only speculate whether his career would have survived the coming of talking pictures. In 1926, Warner Brothers introduced a sound system called Vitaphone, which electronically synchronized the motion picture image with a phonographic recording of the soundtrack. When Al Jolson broke into song onscreen in *The Jazz Singer* (1927), it marked the beginning of the end of the silent film. Many silent stars were quickly retired. Heavy accents or effete voices wouldn't record well, and there was no turning back to the days of the silent screen.

Ever resilient, the film industry weathered the transition to sound. The Academy of Motion Picture Arts and Sciences formed and began giving out annual awards for excellence. The first Best Picture award went to the World War I flying drama, *Wings*. Two years later, the 1929 stock market crash plunged the country into the Great Depression. The film community braced itself for what the thirties might bring.

Greta Garbo, cast by Louis B. Mayer in Torrent *(1926), her first American film.*

The end of the silent era — Al Jolson in The Jazz Singer *(1927) — the first talkie.*

Wings (1927) won the first Best Picture Academy Award.

GARY COOPER

Cooper as a cowboy stuntman in 1925, when he broke into the movies.

Cooper's first major role — as Abe Lee (far right) in The Winning of Barbara Worth *(1926), starring Vilma Bánky and Ronald Colman.*

He made a career out of calm, and he could speak volumes with just a few words and a nod. But Gary Cooper had a wild, physical side. In his early career he was a stunt man in silent westerns. It wasn't surprising that he had his own doubts about his career when talkies arrived. After all, when sound became a part of the equation, Cooper's rugged frontiersman physique and his agility in the saddle could no longer speak to audiences in the same way. As he would say, he'd have to do it a newfangled way. But he was unflappable in the face of obstacles and used to adapting to foreign ways.

Cooper grew up with his feet firmly planted in two worlds: the Big Sky Country of his father's Montana and the genteel British society of his illness-prone mother. Born May 7, 1901, in Helena, Montana, Frank Gary Cooper spent his earliest years on the family ranch before moving to England with his ailing mother at age five. Determined to mold her son into the image of a proper English gentleman, Cooper's mother enrolled him in an exclusive school, but the growing threat of World War I forced mother and son to return to the safety of the family's Montana ranch.

Once he recovered from the culture shock of living back in the States, Cooper again left Montana to attend Iowa's Grinnell College, where he studied art. Although he dabbled in acting, appearing in several college productions, Cooper was more intent on becoming a political cartoonist. When it became clear that he couldn't support himself as a cartoonist, Cooper headed to California to break into the movies. A skilled rider, he initially found work as a stunt man on several westerns.

Cooper's first break came from an unexpected source — his lawyer father, who had recently been named a judge. When he moved to California, the younger Cooper hadn't informed his parents that he had acting ambitions. He feared that they would think him frivolous and a failure, unlike his brother, who had become a successful financier. But when his parents announced that they would be in California on business, he felt he had to break the news. He asked only for their emotional support, not realizing how wide his father's network of contacts was.

In 1926, Cooper was hired to play the lead in an upcoming two-reel featurette. The offer came from a Colonel Ford, a low-budget producer whose finances were managed by Cooper's father. The film, titled *Lightnin' Wins* (1926), is a simplistic western that was conceived primarily as a vehicle for starlet Eileen Sedgwick. Cooper's role, while nominally the male lead, is mostly an afterthought, but it didn't feel that way to Cooper. During a rushed two days of shooting, he was hardly able to control his nerves, which resulted in a severely exaggerated performance (though it did persuade Cooper's mother that he was a born actor). Barely released to theaters, *Lightnin' Wins* did little to advance Cooper's career, though Colonel Ford assured him that there might be other opportunities down the road.

Fortunately, Cooper's father once again came to his aid. Through another elaborate web of connections, Judge Cooper negotiated a minor role for his son as the villain in a feature called *Tricks,* which was designed to showcase "the beautiful Marilyn Mills" and her pair of trick horses. While Cooper doesn't come across as a very threatening bad guy, the picture's leading lady thought Cooper had an "interesting" face and put him in touch with his first agent, Nan Collins. Collins was the one who suggested changing his name to Gary — after her hometown in Indiana — instead of the overly common Frank.

After another year of work as a stunt man and bit player, Gary Cooper landed a meaty supporting role in *The Winning of Barbara Worth* (1926), starring Ronald Colman and Hungarian siren Vilma Bánky. When the actor originally hired to play Colman's rival for Bánky dropped out of the project, Cooper stepped into the role of Abe Lee, the ill-fated ranch foreman who dies in a dam explosion. Colman had top billing, but it was the handsome, laconic Cooper who most impressed audiences and critics with his unaffected presence. Variety's film critic wrote, "Cooper is a youth who will be heard of on the screen." He would, in fact, go on to become the dominant romantic hero in American cinema for the next two decades.

"Cooper is a youth who will be heard of on the screen."

— *Variety* on
Cooper's first major role

GRETA GARBO

Her striking, classical beauty almost instantly drew attention in her first featured role in *The Atonement of Gosta Berling* (1924). From then on, and throughout her career from the silent films of the late twenties to the early talkies of the thirties, Garbo gradually captured the public's imagination with her elusiveness and emotional reserve. She has long inspired writers to describe her mysterious allure. Playwright Clare Boothe Luce wrote that Greta Garbo was "a deer in the body of a woman living resentfully in the Hollywood zoo."

Long before she was the hypnotic Garbo, the screen siren was simply Greta Lovisa Gustafsson: a pretty lather girl in a Stockholm barbershop. Born on September 18, 1905, she grew up in precarious circumstances, due to her father's alcoholism. His death thrust the family even deeper into poverty, forcing teenaged Greta to leave school and work, first in a barbershop and then as a salesgirl at a local department store. Luckily for the aspiring actress, the enterprising owner of the store regularly made short promotional films featuring the prettiest salesgirls touting store merchandise. Garbo's coyness and girlish figure registered strongly with the films' producer, who hired her to appear in several of them.

Heartened by her string of small successes, Garbo pursued a scholarship to drama school and won. She also played a small role in the comedy short *Peter The Tramp* (1922), in which she frolics lakeside in a bathing suit. The film did little to advance her career, so she threw herself back into her studies at the Royal Dramatic Theater. It was there that she met the virtuoso film director, Mauritz Stiller.

At the time, Stiller was looking for an unknown actress to play the lead in his ambitious epic, *The Atonement of Gosta Berling*. He interviewed one of Garbo's fellow students for the part first, but found her style too polished and her beauty too conventional. When Garbo arrived for her interview with Stiller, she was flushed with excitement. In her naïveté and especially in her expressive eyes, Stiller saw exactly the qualities he hoped to capture in his heroine, Countess Elizabeth Dohna. Unfortunately, Garbo's inexperience was painfully evident in her stiff audition for the role.

Most of Stiller's assistants thought it foolish to cast her in such a major role, but Stiller had enormous faith in his discovery's hidden talents. Changing her last name to Garbo, Stiller trained his young star with alternating toughness and indulgence, stretching her to the very limits of her capabilities. With Stiller's exacting standards, filming one scene could take several agonizing days, and Garbo, who was only eighteen, almost cracked under the pressure. But Swedish film critics widely recognized the results as magnificent. Garbo's performance as the countess who becomes the obsession of an alcoholic priest is deeply affecting.

While not a blockbuster, *The Atonement of Gosta Berling* brought both Garbo and Stiller to the attention of MGM executive Louis B. Mayer, who signed them to a studio contract. Garbo was an immediate sensation in her first American film, *Torrent* (1926). Unlike many of the era's screen sirens, she neither vamps nor flirts with her leading man, Ricardo Cortez. She instead suggests the passion simmering beneath the surface, especially in the intense love scenes.

With her Swedish accent, Garbo may have appeared doomed when talkies arrived, but her husky voice only enhanced her image. She made a triumphant sound debut as the title character in *Anna Christie* (1930), winning an Oscar nomination for her role as the world-weary prostitute. She would remain a top star until her abrupt retirement in 1941.

"A deer in the body of a woman living resentfully in the Hollywood zoo."

— playwright Clare Boothe Luce

A young Swedish schoolgirl — Garbo at the age of ten.

Garbo made her U.S. screen debut in MGM's Torrent *(1926) — a performance that wowed the MGM brass.*

RUDOLPH VALENTINO

Female moviegoers literally swooned over Valentino; his heavy-lidded, smoldering gaze spoke of passion and romance.

Valentino as Dick Bradley in *A Society Sensation* (1918) — his first credited movie role.

Valentino in *The Four Horsemen of the Apocalypse* (1921), his first feature film. The movie made him a Hollywood sensation.

He sprang onto the screen like some character from a dime store romance novel. Darkly handsome and seductive, Valentino introduced the "latin lover" archetype to twenties movie audiences and inspired a fanatical following among women. He was an object of desire, an exotic, uninhibited performer who carried himself with the sinuous grace of a dancer. His stylized, highly theatrical acting is now the stuff of easy caricature, but for all his nostril flaring and posing, Valentino is one of the silent screen's most enduring mythical figures.

To enhance Valentino's exotic appeal, early press releases described him as a poor street urchin who left Italy to seek his fortune in America. Aside from the fact that he was from Italy, the rest of this account is pure fiction. Rodolfo Alfonzo Raffaele Pierre Filibert Guglielmi was born on May 6, 1895, in Castellaneta, Italy, to a veterinarian and the daughter of a French surgeon. He grew up in a comfortable, middle-class household and left for America in 1913 after completing his studies at a nearby agricultural college.

Arriving in New York, Valentino spent his days as a gardener's assistant and his nights dancing at the posh nightclub, Maxim's. His dancing won him a spot in a touring company, which ultimately brought him to southern California. In 1917 Valentino made his screen debut as an extra in a ballroom sequence in the film, *Alimony.* Going by the name M. Rudolpho De Valentina, he subsequently found additional film work as an extra or as the swarthy villain for the next few years until screenwriter June Mathis saw his leading-man potential. She was then writing the script for *The Four Horsemen of the Apocalypse* and convinced director Rex Ingram to cast Valentino as Julio Desnoyers, the ne'er-do-well grandson of a rich Argentinian cattle baron. In the role of the spoiled playboy who'd rather tango than work, Valentino was a sensation. His sultry, passionate tango with co-star Beatrice Dominguez is a highlight of the film, which follows Julio to Paris and eventual redemption as a brave soldier in World War I.

Female moviegoers literally swooned over Valentino; his heavy-lidded, smoldering gaze spoke of passion and romance. The last vestiges of prim Victorian morality were disappearing, allowing women in the early twenties to savor a newfound freedom. Valentino's allure thus held a special fascination for many, who turned out in droves to see him ravish his willing co-star, Agnes Ayres, in *The Sheik* (1921).

Over the next five years, Valentino played basically the same role with only slight variations in fourteen more films. Married twice, the first time reportedly only for a matter of hours, Valentino was dominated by his second wife Natacha Rambova, an art director whose real name was Winifred Hudnut. A pretentious, controlling woman, Rambova was eventually banned from the set of Valentino's films. Following the premiere of *Son of the Sheik* (1926) Valentino collapsed. He died eight days later from peritonitis at the age of thirty-one. Reports following the announcement indicated that a number of women around the world chose suicide rather than to live in a world without their beloved Valentino.

OTHER STARS OF THE PERIOD

Louise Briooks   *Joan Crawford*   *Stan Laurel and Oliver Hardy*   *Fredric March*

Clara Bow got her start when she won a movie magazine's beauty contest, which then led to a bit part in a film. With her bobbed hair, flashing eyes, and boundless energy, she became the screen's reigning flapper — the "it" girl of the Jazz Age who flagrantly danced the Charleston and swigged bathtub gin. In 1922, Bow made her first two films — *Beyond the Rainbow* and *Down to the Sea in Ships*, but her big break came in 1927 when she was cast as a shopgirl in *It*, a movie based on the writings of British novelist Elinor Glyn.

Louise Brooks started dancing professionally with the Ziegfeld Follies at age fifteen. In 1925 she played a bit part in *The Street of Forgotten Men*. She made her first appearance as a flapper in the comedy *The American Venus* (1926). With her modern beauty and sleek, bobbed hair, Brooks projects an erotic and understated allure. A brilliant, headstrong woman who made no secret of her contempt for Hollywood, she jumped at the chance to play Lulu, the amoral temptress in G.W. Pabst's *Pandora's Box* (1929), which was filmed in Berlin. When she returned to America, however, Brooks was considered a has-been and retired after a few minor roles in low-budget films. All but forgotten, Brooks was rediscovered by film historians in the fifties, who hailed her performances for Pabst in both *Pandora's Box* and *Diary of a Lost Girl* (1929) as screen acting at its finest.

Joan Crawford was born Lucille Fay Le Sueur in San Antonio, Texas. Odd jobs as a shopgirl, waitress, and laundress preceded her earliest show business success as a dancer. She was discovered in a Broadway chorus line and immediately signed to a contract with MGM. To create publicity for the young actress, the studio launched a nationwide search for a new stage name. "Joan Crawford" was born and remained a Hollywood icon for nearly five decades, moving seamlessly from silent films to talkies. Her first role was a bit part in *Pretty Ladies* in 1925, but it wasn't until 1928 that she reached star status for her lead in *Our Dancing Daughters*.

Stan Laurel and **Oliver Hardy** didn't team up until 1927, when they appeared together in *Duck Soup*. But their careers started long before that, with both actors appearing independently in a variety of shorts. Hardy debuted in *Outwitting Dad* (1914) and Laurel in *Nuts In May* (1917). Coincidentally, the two actually appeared together for the first time in the 1917 short *Lucky Dog*, but not as a team. It would be years later that director Leo McCarey convinced the actors to perform together on a regular basis. The rest, of course, is history. The duo starred in more than a hundred films, most of them short subjects, including the Oscar-winning *The Music Box* (1932).

Fredric March, born Ernest Frederick McIntyre, studied drama at the University of Wisconsin after serving during World War I. He headed to New York to be a banker, but the lure of the theater proved greater than the lure of money. He started acting in small stage productions before graduating to the silver screen. In 1929, March made his film debut in the kidnapping drama, *The Dummy*. March followed this with a wickedly funny parody of John Barrymore in *The Royal Family of Broadway* (1930), which brought him his first Oscar nomination. He alternated between film and theater over the next few years, with his most successful role coming in the 1931 film *Dr. Jekyll and Mr. Hyde,* for which he won an Oscar. He eventually won another Oscar in 1947 for his part in *The Best Years of Our Lives* (1946).

Clara Bow

1930-1939

THE GOLDEN AGE OF THE MOVIES

With the nation plunged into the most profound economic depression it had ever known, millions of Americans sought a means of escape at the local movie theater from the crushing pressure of day-to-day survival. For the price of one thin dime, weary audiences could see Shirley Temple as Heidi dancing in the Swiss Alps or Judy Garland skipping down a yellow brick road. And for those seeking deeper cinematic fare, there was Gary Cooper and Clark Gable.

Through the alchemy of cinematic genius, the silver screen turned to gold. The offering of films was arguably among the greatest of all time. By now movies had become a driving force in western culture.

At first, however, the Crash affected the film industry. Movie attendance dropped and studios were forced to lay off many workers. To counteract this trend, theater owners introduced the double feature: two films were shown for the price of one admission, with a low-budget B-movie playing second to the "A" main feature.

With the advent of the talkies, many silent film stars suddenly found themselves reduced to has-beens almost overnight. Eager to fill the void, the studios turned to Broadway for talent. Stage-trained actors such as James Cagney, Katharine Hepburn, Bette Davis, Fredric March, and Humphrey Bogart came to Hollywood as new genres sprang up — the musical, the screwball comedy, and the gangster film. The violence and blatant sexuality spurred the formation of the Motion Picture Production Code in 1934. Studios submitted all scripts to this organization, whose members eliminated any overt references to violence, sexuality, drug use, and other social taboos.

During the thirties, each studio became known for a particular genre and style of filmmaking. MGM celebrated middle-class values and had a certain brightness and opulence. And it certainly had the stars: Joan Crawford, Clark Gable, Myrna Loy, William Powell, Greta Garbo, Norma Shearer, Jean Harlow, Mickey Rooney, Judy Garland, as well as directors King Vidor, Victor Fleming, and George Cukor.

Warner Brothers was chiefly known for its gritty, socially themed melodramas and gangster films. James Cagney, Bette Davis, Edward G. Robinson, and George Raft were on the studio's talent roster. The studio also hired choreographer Busby Berkeley, whose precision-choreographed, visually striking dance sequences in films like *Footlight Parade* (1933) skirt the boundary between innovation and camp. And RKO could claim one of the greatest movie dancers of all time — Broadway veteran Fred Astaire.

Bogie left Broadway in 1930 to sign a film contract with Hollywood's 20th Century Fox.

James Cagney's first film, Sinner's Holiday (1930), released by Warner Bros.

Bela Lugosi in Dracula (1931).

Classic gangster film, Scarface (1932), starring Paul Muni with George Raft.

Paramount Studios was known for its sophisticated light comedies with stars such as Marlene Dietrich, Gary Cooper, Cary Grant, Fredric March, and director Ernst Lubitsch.

Universal made B-movies, specializing in horror. The studio released *Dracula* and *Frankenstein* in 1931, followed by *The Mummy* in 1932, making stars out of Bela Lugosi and Boris Karloff.

Perhaps the preeminent male star of the decade, however, was Clark Gable. Sparks flew whether he was paired with Norma Shearer, Joan Crawford, or Greta Garbo. A string of strong films culminated in the Academy Award-winning *Gone With the Wind* at decade's end. The top-drawing female star from 1935 to 1938 was 20th Century Fox's Shirley Temple. The precociously talented child star was a box office tonic during the dark days of the Depression.

The advent of sound reinvigorated the comedy film. The Marx Brothers made some of their best films during the thirties: *Animal Crackers* (1930), *Horse Feathers* (1932), *Duck Soup* (1933), and *A Night at the Opera* (1935). With their rapid-fire dialogue, comedy classics *Twentieth Century* (1934), *My Man Godfrey* (1936), and *Bringing Up Baby* (1938) set a standard for romantic comedy that endures to this day.

The 1930s ended with what many consider the greatest single year in the history of filmmaking. In 1939, *Gone With the Wind*, *The Wizard of Oz*, *Stagecoach*, *Mr. Smith Goes to Washington*, *Wuthering Heights*, *Destry Rides Again*, and *Dark Victory* were released to critical and commercial acclaim. Hollywood had survived the Depression to emerge triumphant by decade's end.

Paramount assembled a blockbuster cast for Now and Forever (1934) — Carole Lombard, Shirley Temple, and Gary Cooper.

Throughout the decade, the provocative Mae West pushed the boundaries of cinematic sexuality.

FRED ASTAIRE

The movies' first and possibly greatest dance star was born Frederic Austerlitz Jr. on May 10, 1899, in Omaha, Nebraska. When he and his older sister Adele showed a gift for dancing, Astaire's theatrical-minded mother moved with the children to New York City. Adopting their grandmother's maiden name, Astaire, the siblings learned to combine tap dancing with ballroom dancing under the direction of instructor Ned Wayburn. In 1917, they made their Broadway debut in *Over the Top* at the grand opening of the Theater on the Roof. In no time, the Astaires became the toast of musical theater on Broadway and abroad, where they socialized with European royalty.

"Can't sing. Can't act. Slightly balding. Can dance a little."

— A Paramount talent scout on Astaire's first screen test

Astaire performed on stage in both the
United States and Britain before
breaking into film. Here
he is on a New York
City dock in 1930 —
three years before
he made his
screen debut.

In 1928, a scout for Paramount asked them to do a screen test. When nothing came of it, the Astaires shrugged it off and continued with their theatrical engagements. Only later would they learn that while producers felt Adele Astaire had big screen potential as a solo performer, Fred was summarily dismissed with the following shortsighted critique: "Can't sing. Can't act. Slightly balding. Can dance a little."

The act broke up in 1932 when Adele got married and retired to Ireland with her new husband. Without a partner, Astaire continued to work on Broadway, but his thoughts turned more and more often to Hollywood. He worked with agent Leland Hayward to contact David O. Selznick, the head of RKO at the time. Impressed with his work on the stage, Selznick felt that Astaire had great potential to succeed in musical comedies — if he looked good on the screen test. But the 1933 test was not much better than its predecessor, prompting Selznick to comment on Astaire's "enormous ears and bad chin line." The studio was indecisive so Astaire remained with *The Gay Divorcee* on stage.

When Selznick suddenly left RKO for MGM, director Mark Sandrich encouraged RKO to sign Astaire. He felt that the future of movies was in musicals — and Fred Astaire was a natural. Astaire was signed for a supporting role in *Flying Down to Rio* (1933) at the rate of $1,500 a week. Since filming was not scheduled to begin until August, Selznick again jumped on the bandwagon and borrowed Astaire for a bit part in an MGM musical called *Dancing Lady* (1933), starring Clark Gable and Joan Crawford. A vanity piece for Crawford, the movie features Astaire in three scenes: a short rehearsal routine and two song-and-dance numbers. A veteran trouper, he performs ably and makes Crawford look good.

With no time to reflect on his first job, Astaire was thrust into his second film: it was time to shoot RKO's *Flying Down to Rio*, starring Dolores Del Rio and Gene Raymond. Fifth-billed Astaire plays an accordionist who trades wisecracks with a fellow supporting player, a tart blonde named Ginger Rogers. Ostensibly cast as comic relief, Astaire and Rogers effectively steal the movie, dancing a sultry tango called "The Carioca." Any doubts the film's producers may have had about Astaire's screen prospects vanished when they discovered his talent for comedy and his better-than-average singing ability. They knew from the start that he could dance; what they didn't expect was the potent, sexy chemistry that Astaire and Rogers generate in their two-minute-long dance number. A smash success that saved RKO from bankruptcy, *Flying Down to Rio* elevated Astaire from the ranks of supporting player to marquee attraction.

Astaire with
leading lady
Joan Crawford
on the set of his
feature film debut,
Dancing Lady (1933).

(facing page) Astaire with longtime
dance partner Ginger Rogers in one of
their earliest pairings — 1934's
The Gay Divorcee.

HUMPHREY BOGART

A budding star — Bogart at age two.

One of the earliest Bogart films, John Ford's Up the River *(1930), debuted another newcomer, Spencer Tracy (right).*

Born a rich kid, he made his mark in the early thirties playing tough guys and criminals. The hard-boiled, sardonic anti-hero who bucks the system to follow his own moral code, "Bogie" is one of the truly mythic figures of popular culture. Although he played both romantic leads and vicious criminals over the course of his long career, Bogart chiefly endures as the archetypal private eye of film noir: the cynical, brooding loner who maintains his integrity in a morally ambivalent world.

Born in 1899 to a Manhattan surgeon and a magazine illustrator, Humphrey DeForest Bogart seemingly had little or no inclination to fulfill parental expectations. A rebellious student with mediocre grades, he was expelled from New England's prestigious Phillips Academy his senior year. Rejecting his father's wishes that he become a physician, Bogart instead joined the Navy toward the end of World War I. At war's end, he returned to New York, where he began working as a stage manager for a theatrical company. In time he moved from backstage to the footlights. Though never a matinee idol, Bogart nonetheless worked steadily on Broadway until 1930, when Fox signed him to a film contract.

The birth of the talkies had been the professional death knell for many silent film greats. Anxious to find new stars, the studios scoured Broadway for camera-ready talent. Like his contemporaries James Cagney and Edward G. Robinson, Bogart didn't fit the conventional mold of a movie star. But while Cagney and Robinson found their signature roles early in *The Public Enemy* (1931) and *Little Caesar* (1930), respectively, Bogart made an inauspicious debut in the now-forgotten *A Devil With Women* (1930).

The film pairs Bogart with character actor Victor McLaglen in an early buddy comedy set in Central America. Bogart plays Tom Standish, the wisecracking, spoiled rich kid who hooks up with McLaglen's Jerry Maxton, a crusty soldier of fortune. As revolution sweeps the country, the comically mismatched duo runs afoul of everyone, usually because of Bogart's antics. Deliverance arrives in the form of a beautiful señorita played by Luana Alañiz, who not only helps them escape but also falls for Bogart, much to McLaglen's chagrin.

Although Bogart received decent notices for the film, he was neither handsome nor suave enough to make it as a leading man in the era of Cary Grant and Gary Cooper. He instead found steady employment as a supporting player in Warner Brothers crime melodramas. Unhappy with the caliber of his film work, Bogart returned to Broadway to play escaped criminal Duke Mantee, opposite Leslie Howard, in Robert Sherwood's drama *The Petrified Forest*. After years of languishing in routine films, Bogart had finally found a role worthy of his talents. Yet when it came time to cast the film version of the play, Warner Brothers initially vetoed him in favor of box office draw Edward G. Robinson. Only co-star Leslie Howard's intervention with the studio brass on his behalf gave Bogart his much-needed second shot in Hollywood. Opposite Howard and Bette Davis in the 1936 film, Bogart impressed moviegoers and critics as the ruthless convict holding the customers of an Arizona diner hostage. While a success, *The Petrified Forest* inexplicably failed to catapult Bogart to the front ranks of cinema "tough guys." It would be five long years before Bogart found his career-defining role: Sam Spade, the detective hero of Dashiell Hammett's *The Maltese Falcon* (1941).

Again, Humphrey Bogart wasn't the studio's first choice. In what must rank as one of the worst career decisions in Hollywood history, George Raft turned down the film because

he reportedly didn't want to work with John Huston, a screenwriter making his directorial debut. In fact, Bogart was twice the beneficiary of Raft's bad career decisions; he had earlier replaced Raft in Raoul Walsh's *High Sierra* (1941). The combination of Huston, Bogart, and Hammett proved irresistible to moviegoers. A critical and commercial success, *The Maltese Falcon* effectively heralded the long-overdue arrival of Humphrey Bogart as a bona fide movie star and box office draw, a position he would maintain until his death in 1957.

The cynical brooding loner who maintains his integrity in a morally ambivalent world

JAMES CAGNEY

"**M**ade it, Ma. Top of the world!" Thus Cody Jarrett, played by James Cagney, in *White Heat* (1949) — one of the most quoted lines in film history. Cagney was a truly unique star, one who could convincingly play both a mother-fixated psychopath and a patriotic song-and-dance man (in *Yankee Doodle Dandy*). Versatility was what made him a standout in a screen career that spanned half a century.

The scrappy, energetic performer with a trademark staccato delivery was a product of New York's tough Lower East Side. "Jimmy," as he was affectionately known, was born to an Irish father and Norwegian mother on July 17, 1899. As a child, he aspired to become an artist. The family's financial woes, however, ultimately forced him to put that "folly" aside and work a variety of odd jobs, from poolroom racker to female impersonator in a Yorkville review. His days in rouge and high heels were mercifully short-lived; in 1920, he landed a spot in the chorus of the Broadway musical *Pitter-Patter*. Stints in vaudeville followed, and by the mid-twenties Cagney had graduated from bit parts to leading roles. His performance in the musical, *Penny Arcade,* brought him to Hollywood, where he recreated the part in the Warner Brothers film version, retitled *Sinner's Holiday* (1930).

With a running time of just under an hour, *Sinner's Holiday* features Cagney as Harry Delano, the quick-tempered son of a penny arcade owner. After he accidentally kills his partner in a rum-running business, Cagney schemes to pin the murder on an innocent carnival barker. Cliché-ridden even by the standards of the day, *Sinner's Holiday* nonetheless secured Cagney a place in the Warner Brothers company of players. A handful of roles in negligible films followed before maverick director William Wellman picked Cagney to play the upstart gangster Tom Powers in *The Public Enemy* (1931).

A hard-hitting, unsentimental depiction of organized crime in Prohibition-era Chicago, *The Public Enemy* shocked audiences with its unflinching brutality. For Cagney, it was a role that tapped into his nervous, mercurial energy; vulnerable one moment, he turns cruel in an instant, smashing a half-grapefruit into Mae Clarke's face in a now-classic scene.

Cagney quickly became the studio's newest star. Invariably cast as the rough-hewn Irish "tough guy" in subsequent films, however, he grew weary of the role and took parts that enabled him to stretch; as a Broadway producer in the musical *Footlight Parade* (1933), Cagney even gets the chance to tap dance opposite Ruby Keeler. He also took a crack at Shakespeare, playing Bottom in Max Reinhardt's all-star adaptation of *A Midsummer Night's Dream* (1935), which also features a very young Mickey Rooney as Puck.

Although he left Warner Brothers in the mid-thirties to set up his own production company with his brother William, Cagney returned to the studio fold after producing and starring in two box office disappointments, *Great Guy* (1936), and *Something To Sing About* (1937). Cagney soon bounced back with the gangster drama *Angels With Dirty Faces* (1938), which brought him his first Oscar nomination. His career upswing continued with the gangster epic *The Roaring Twenties* (1939).

From 1939 through his final screen appearance in Milos Forman's *Ragtime* (1981), Cagney worked in virtually every film genre: comedy, action, musical, crime drama; he even saddled up for a 1939 western co-starring Humphrey Bogart, *The Oklahoma Kid*. Much imitated but never duplicated, Cagney is a true original whose appeal remains undimmed.

Cagney was a truly unique star, one who could convincingly play both a mother-fixated psychopath and a patriotic song-and-dance man.

A young James Francis Cagney Jr. at the turn of the century.

Cagney opposite Joan Blondell in his film debut, Sinner's Holiday (1930).

BING CROSBY

*Crosby
at age eighteen
as a freshman at Gonzaga University.*

Crosby (far left), as a member of The Rhythm Boys, made his feature-film debut in The King of Jazz (1930).

Crosby may not have been strikingly handsome, but his easygoing charm and casual style garnered attention in his very first film, *The King of Jazz* (1930), even though his minor role as a band singer was not credited. Ironically, when audiences began to recognize the unidentified, curly-topped crooner in other early films, he'd merely been playing himself, an unknown singer, too insignificant to make the movie credits as a real character. Though audiences warmed up to him almost at the outset, nearly a decade would pass before he hit his stride.

Nicknamed "Bing" after the hero of the comic strip *The Bingville Bungle,* Harry Lillis Crosby was born on May 2, 1903, in Tacoma, Washington, the fourth of seven children in a musical household. A drummer and singer, Crosby dutifully entered Gonzaga University to study law, but he was far more interested in becoming a professional singer. He dropped out of college to form The Rhythm Boys with Al Rinker and Harris Barris. By 1928, they were singing with the renowned Paul Whiteman Band.

Crosby was fortunate to be in the right place at the right time. Earlier singers had been forced to belt out songs to project to their audiences. The advent of the microphone allowed Crosby to sing his tunes softly and intimately, a style that he made famous as "crooning." Movie mogul Mack Sennett caught his act at the Coconut Grove in 1931 and said, "What struck me about this guy was that all the stuffed shirts at the Grove stopped dancing and gathered around the bandstand to watch him croon. He held them."

By the time Sennett caught his act, Crosby had already made his screen debut with Whiteman and The Rhythm Boys in the lavish musical revue *The King of Jazz* (1930). The night before he was scheduled to sing a solo in the film, Crosby had had a few too many drinks at a party. A traffic accident on his way home resulted in a drunk-driving charge and a day in jail. Although Crosby returned to the set in time to sing with the band, he found his solo had been reassigned to John Boles.

Crosby would later get a solo number in *Reaching for the Moon* (1930). A shipboard romance starring Douglas Fairbanks Jr., the film features Crosby and The Rhythm Boys as the ship's entertainment. His film career later received a much-needed boost from Sennett, who signed him to star in a series of six twenty-minute musical comedy shorts. Crosby's success in these shorts led to a 1931 radio show for CBS that was heard around America — and brought him instant fame.

Hoping to capitalize on the singer's radio success, Paramount signed him for *The Big Broadcast* (1932). Crosby plays himself, teaming up with friends to save a failing radio station. A strange curio of a movie, *The Big Broadcast* is an uneasy blend of musical numbers, comedy, and melodrama. Despondent when his girlfriend dumps him, Crosby invites co-star Stu Erwin to join him in a suicide pact. They turn on the gas and shut the windows and wait for death, as a ghostly accordion player hovers in the background, playing "Here Lies Love." Thanks to a worried neighbor, the two survive for the requisite happy ending.

Primarily a vehicle to showcase the talents of Crosby and other radio stars like Kate Smith and Burns and Allen, *The Big Broadcast* opened to respectable, if not spectacular, notices. But within two years, Crosby would make the first of many appearances in the top ten list of box office stars.

BETTE DAVIS

Davis was initially dismissed by Universal as "having about as much sex appeal as Slim Summerville," a lanky, hayseed character actor of the era.

Bette Davis (left), as a youngster, with her sister Bobbie.

Davis, flanked by a young Humphrey Bogart (left) and her co-star Conrad Nagel, makes her screen debut in 1931's The Bad Sister.

Davis would have been the first to admit —and probably boast —that she was never considered a Hollywood glamour girl. A tough-minded, acerbic actress, she was initially dismissed by Universal as "having about as much sex appeal as Slim Summerville," a lanky hayseed character actor of the era. But audiences have viewed her bravura acting and mesmerizing gaze differently.

At a time when most stars shied away from playing unlikable characters, Davis aggressively lobbied for the role of Mildred, the slatternly Cockney waitress who torments the sensitive hero in *Of Human Bondage* (1934). Her daring performance led to a write-in campaign on her behalf for the Academy Award for Best Actress. Although she lost to Claudette Colbert, Davis finally became one of Warner Brothers' top stars. It had been a four-year journey for the actress, whose unconventional appeal and imperious attitude are now the stuff of Hollywood legend.

Like fellow New Englander Katharine Hepburn, Davis had a formidable mother who raised her daughter to be an independent, forthright woman. A child of divorce, Ruth Elizabeth Davis was born on April 5, 1908, in Lowell, Massachusetts, and originally planned to become a dancer. This all changed, however, when she discovered acting in high school. After graduating from the Cushing Academy, Davis auditioned for a position in Eva LeGallienne's famed Manhattan Civic Repertory. Unfortunately, she was rejected for being "too frivolous and insincere." With the resilience that later bore her through many professional and personal disappointments, Davis shrugged this off and enrolled in John Murray Anderson's Dramatic School. She quickly became the star pupil, eclipsing a fellow student named Lucille Ball.

Upon graduation, Davis joined a Rochester, New York, repertory company headed by George Cukor, but her forceful personality and tendency for overdramatizing led to her dismissal from the troupe. Taking her rejection in stride, Davis went on to land her first professional role in the off-Broadway production of *The Earth Between*. A tour of two plays followed, and in 1929 she starred in the Broadway comedy, *Broken Dishes.*

A hit with audiences and critics, Davis caught the eye of Samuel Goldwyn's talent scout, who arranged a screen test. After screening the results, studio executives rejected Davis, claiming she had little glamour and no sex appeal. Her second screen test for Universal elicited the same reaction. Fortunately, Davis found a champion in talent scout David Warner, who assured the young actress that they could fix her up once she got to Hollywood. It may not have been much of a recommendation, but it was a start —and Davis began her film career at $300 a week.

While Davis later made her mark playing strong women, her film debut in *The Bad Sister* in 1931 is uncharacteristically subdued. Lead actress Sydney Fox completely overshadows Davis, who plays the heroine's dowdy sister, Laura Madison. When Laura's older sister Marianne falls for a con man (played by newcomer Humphrey Bogart) and leaves town, Laura finally wins the heart of her sister's former beau, Dr. Lindley. Silent film star Conrad Nagel, who played Lindley, later recalled Davis as being very shy and insecure, probably because she was well aware that the studio was less than enamored with her talents.

Even *Variety*'s favorable review of her performance was not enough to bolster her confidence. Only photographer Karl Freund recognized Davis's screen potential, asserting: "she has lovely eyes." The movie was largely ignored by the public and panned by the

studio, which ultimately dropped her contract after a couple of other minor films.

Discouraged and out of work, Davis was about to leave Hollywood when she was signed by Warner Brothers The studio, which specialized in gangster movies, was happy to have an actress to use in a variety of female roles. It was while working for Warner that Davis finally gave in to the fad of the day and dyed her hair blonde.

Her first role for the studio was in *The Man Who Played God* in 1932. As the fiancée of a concert pianist who loses his hearing, Davis delivers the first of many inspiring performances. It was a momentary respite from the formulaic, often B-movie material that Warner Brothers assigned her. Two years and several films later, Davis would finally become a star in RKO's *Of Human Bondage*.

Davis in a 1932 publicity shot.

HENRY FONDA

From the beginning of his film career in the mid-1930s, Henry Fonda's down-home yet heroic style earned him a reputation in Hollywood as singularly American. It was no surprise that John Ford cast him in the title role of *Young Mr. Lincoln* (1939) and as Tom Joad in *The Grapes of Wrath* (1940). Over the course of his long career, Fonda often played ordinary men of principle who risk everything to stand up to oppression or prejudice.

Acting was not on Fonda's radar growing up in rural Grand Island, Nebraska. Born May 16, 1905, to a printer and his wife, Fonda was a gifted writer who won a short story contest at the age of ten and planned to become a newspaper reporter. He went on to attend the University of Minnesota, where he paid his tuition by coaching children at the Unity Settlement House. Mentally and physically exhausted from juggling college and work, however, Fonda flunked out in his sophomore year after he drew pictures in his final exam blue books.

Adrift, Fonda returned home to Nebraska, where his mother's friend convinced him to join the Omaha Community Playhouse. That friend was Dorothy Brando, whose baby son Marlon would ultimately follow Fonda into acting. Quiet and shy, he was initially terrified of appearing on a stage — until he did it the first time. There, in Omaha, the magic struck and Fonda decided to become an actor.

Not long after his local stage debut, a neighbor needed a ride to Cape Cod. Fonda agreed to drive her, hoping to find work at an East Coast theater. He found an opening at a summer stock company called University Players in 1928, where he met lifelong friends Jimmy Stewart and Margaret Sullavan, to whom Fonda was briefly married in the early thirties. The couple divorced amicably and later worked together onscreen in the screwball comedy *The Moon's Our Home* (1936).

He remained with the group for several years before turning his sights to Broadway. Subsisting on rice in a tiny New York apartment, Fonda and roommate Jimmy Stewart went on countless auditions. Though he complained that Stewart got all the breaks, Fonda found success on Broadway as well. In 1934 he landed a part in *New Faces of America,* followed by the lead in *The Farmer Takes a Wife* in 1935. As Daniel Harrow, a nineteenth-century farmer forced to work on the river canals, he won both critical praise and Hollywood's attention. When 20th Century Fox acquired the screen rights to the play, Fonda signed on to recreate his role onscreen opposite Janet Gaynor, who was then at the height of her stardom.

It took Fonda a while to adjust to playing for the cameras rather than the last row of the balcony, but once he learned to tone down his delivery, he was a natural in front of the camera. Under Victor Fleming's direction, Fonda and Gaynor get acquainted quite charmingly in this sentimental period romance set on the Erie Canal in the 1850s. That same year, 1935, Fonda starred in two more films: the period romance *Way Down East* and *I Dream Too Much,* a star vehicle for opera diva Lily Pons. Regarding his performances in these films, the *New York Times* called him "the most likeable of the new crop of romantic juveniles." Refusing to be typecast as a romantic leading man, Fonda would soon prove his versatility by tackling roles in everything from screwball comedy to violent crime drama.

Fonda at the age of fourteen.

"The most likeable of the new crop of romantic juveniles."

— *The New York Times* on Fonda's early screen roles

Fonda, reprising his Broadway role, stars opposite Janet Gaynor in The Farmer Takes a Wife (1935), his screen debut.

CLARK GABLE

Gable opposite William Boyd in The Painted Desert (1931), his first talkie.

Gable and co-star Claudette Colbert in the Oscar-winning film It Happened One Night (1934). Both actors also won Academy Awards for their efforts.

In an era when Hollywood's leading men were typically buttoned-down gentlemen, Gable was a brash, audacious man's man. And he didn't exactly turn off women, either. Always commanding, never tentative, Gable, who started in the silents, earned the wings that would take him to filmdom's stratosphere in an early western. A few years after his debut in The Painted Desert (1931), his hold on audiences was so powerful that undershirt sales reportedly dropped precipitously when he removed his dress shirt and stood bare-chested in It Happened One Night (1934).

William Clark Gable was born in 1901 in Cadiz, Ohio, to an oil-field worker and his wife, who died when the star-to-be was just an infant. Always an independent child, he dropped out of high school to work in a tire factory. Escape from the drab tedium of factory work arrived in the form of a local theatrical production, which inspired Gable to pursue acting — a romantic and heady goal for a young man whose bad teeth and large ears diminished his chances to headline, let alone appear onstage. Gable persevered and joined a traveling theatrical company.

What may sound like a colorful, picaresque adventure for an aspiring actor turned out to be a difficult life. Gable was forced to work a series of odd jobs to eke out a living. His luck turned when he met former Broadway actress and teacher Josephine Dillon in 1924. Fourteen years his senior, Dillon saw the potential in the awkward young man so lacking in social graces and poise. She became both his mentor and wife later that year, when the couple moved to Los Angeles.

At Dillon's urging, Gable dropped his first name in favor of Clark, fixed his teeth, and studied etiquette. The mustache was still years away and his ears remained problematic, but Gable was beginning to look more and more like the handsome matinee idol he became a decade later. At this point in his screen career, however, he found only extra work or walk-on roles in a few silent films. With his career stalled and his marriage unraveling towards divorce, Gable returned to the theater and the role of Killer Mears in the prison drama, The Last Mile in Los Angeles. In the role that Spencer Tracy had originated on Broadway, Gable gave a confident and powerful performance as a condemned killer staging a jailbreak. His performance resulted in a flurry of screen tests, but he was turned down by one studio after another. Producer Darryl F. Zanuck dismissed Gable's chances for stardom, saying, "His ears are too big. He looks like an ape."

In 1930, Gable's agent sent him to Pathé Studios for a role in the western, The Painted Desert, starring William Boyd. When asked whether he could ride a horse, he lied and signed up immediately for intensive riding lessons, learning just enough in two weeks to get by. As the villainous Brett, Boyd's romantic rival for the heroine's affections, Gable schemes to eliminate the hero, even blowing up a mine at one point. The loser in the film's climactic showdown, he nonetheless emerged victorious from The Painted Desert — his convincing performance landed him a two-year contract with MGM.

Racking up credits at a dizzying pace, Gable became a fixture in MGM productions, appearing in twelve films in 1931 alone. His gutsy performance opposite Norma Shearer in *A Free Soul* launched him as a full-fledged star. Three years later he won the Academy Award for *It Happened One Night*.

Although it is now inconceivable to picture anyone else in the role, Clark Gable was apparently not writer Margaret Mitchell's first choice to play Rhett Butler in *Gone With the Wind* (1939). She instead preferred the English actor Basil Rathbone, who had recently played the villain opposite Errol Flynn in *The Adventures of Robin Hood* (1938). Fortunately, producer David O. Selznick vetoed Mitchell's choice and went with Gable, the top star of Hollywood's "Golden Age."

"His ears are too big. He looks like an ape."

— Producer Darryl F. Zanuck

JUDY GARLAND

A young Garland, daughter of vaudevillians, on stage just prior to breaking into the movies.

The musical star who was cast in a remake of *A Star is Born* (1954) undoubtedly had a special place in her heart for "Born in a Trunk," a production number from the musical.

She was born Frances Ethel Gumm into a show-business family on June 10, 1922, in Grand Rapids, Minnesota. Her parents were former vaudeville performers who owned a theater, where their two oldest daughters regularly performed as a singing duo. Judy Garland's musical talent manifested itself early, when she toddled onstage to sing "Jingle Bells" with her older sisters. Only two and a half years old, "Baby Gumm" officially became the third member of the touring Gumm Sisters act.

Grand Rapids was too small-time for the Gumms' driven stage mother, who wanted to book her talented daughters into bigger venues. In 1926 the Gumm family moved to Lancaster, California, which became the sisters' launch pad into vaudeville, movie shorts, and the 1934 Chicago World's Fair. It was during the World's Fair that the group came to change their name. When emcee George Jessel introduced the Gumm sisters, many in the audience at the Oriental Theater laughed, assuming it was a comic novelty act. Jessel subsequently took the sisters aside and suggested that they change their last name to Garland. Inspired by a reference to "Judy" in a popular Hoagie Carmichael song, Frances adopted a new first name. Garland later explained that the name sounded peppy and a little bit naughty. Baby Gumm was no more.

In 1935, the Garland Sisters appeared in their last movie short, *La Fiesta de Santa Barbara*. Even though the act broke up later that year when one of the older sisters got married, Judy's mother didn't miss a beat — she simply shifted her attention to managing her youngest daughter's solo career. A number of auditions followed, and Garland got her first break at MGM, signing on for a salary of $100 per week. The thirteen-year-old sang "Zing! Went the Strings of My Heart" accompanied by MGM pianist Roger Edens. He later described her singing as "the biggest thing to happen to the MGM musical." Edens went on to become an influential part of Garland's life.

Garland's first solo film appearance pairs her with teen opera diva and fellow MGM discovery Deanna Durbin. In the MGM short, *Every Sunday* (1936), Durbin sings opera to Garland's swing. Although the short ran in theaters, it was essentially a glorified screen test to help MGM executives decide which actress they wanted to promote. Garland won, but when two studios asked to borrow her, she found herself making her first feature film for 20th Century Fox rather than MGM.

A musical comedy, *Pigskin Parade* (1936), depicts the efforts of a college football coach to recruit a gifted hillbilly for the Yale Bowl. Listed ninth in the cast list, Garland plays the hillbilly's sister, Sairy Dodd, and sings three songs, including the standard "It's Love I'm After." Aside from these musical numbers, she doesn't have

Garland, in her feature film debut — Pigskin Parade (1936), which starred Betty Grable (far left).

much screen time. A critic for the trade newspaper *Daily Variety* nonetheless praised Garland in his review of *Pigskin Parade:* "She's a cute, not too pretty but pleasingly fetching personality, who certainly knows how to sell a pop."

In spite of her golden voice, the powers that be at MGM considered Garland to be little more than a chubby teenager, and her budding career lost steam. Then in 1937, the studio planned a surprise birthday party for their leading male star, Clark Gable. Garland was asked to sing and Edens accompanied her on "You Made Me Love You." She introduced the song as though she were a lovesick fan singing a letter to "Dear Mr. Gable." The song — and the singer — were a hit. She reprised the number in *Broadway Melody of 1938*, her first feature-length film for MGM. Whatever reservations the studio brass had about Garland's screen potential quickly disappeared.

"The biggest thing to happen to the MGM musical."

— Pianist Roger Edens

CARY GRANT

Grant was an actor whose career ingeniously alternated between comedy and serious fare, ranging from domestic dramas like *Penny Serenade* (1941) to the films he made for Alfred Hitchcock. Long before Hitchcock immortalized him, he bore the singularly unwieldy name of Archibald Alexander Leach.

Born on January 18, 1904, in Bristol, England, "Archie," as his contemporaries in Bristol knew him, is regarded as one of the most witty and urbane leading men in film history. He was also a gifted physical comedian, equally skilled at pratfalls and trading barbs with such co-stars as Rosalind Russell and Irene Dunne. The impossibly handsome Grant had no compunction about looking silly or even downright ugly, a quality that sets him apart from other actors in the running for the unofficial designation of the screen's most dashing leading man. His most endearing roles crackle with sexual tension and romantic longing without ever stooping to the obvious – such is the appeal of Grant, whose unflappable charm and irrepressible wit are sorely lacking from contemporary cinema.

Grant, who grew up in abject poverty, also had to contend with his mother's institutionalization when he was nine years old. Devastated, Grant turned to the theater for solace and realized that he'd found his calling. Anxious to leave home, he quit school at fourteen and joined the Bob Pender comedy troupe, in which he danced, did acrobatics, stilt-walked, and performed pantomimes throughout England. In 1920, he was chosen as one of eight troupe members to tour America as the Pender Boys. After 456 performances, Grant chose to stay in America when the troupe dissolved.

Grant's first solo job was stilt-walking with a sandwich board advertising various theaters and cinemas. He then worked his way through bit parts in several small plays before finally winning a credited role in the Broadway play *Golden Dawn*. It was not successful, but it gave him a little name recognition. Grant then appeared in *Boom Boom* in 1929 and *The Street Singer* in 1930. A 20th Century Fox talent scout spotted him in *Boom Boom* and invited him to take a screen test. Unfortunately, the test was not a success — he was told that he was bowlegged and that his neck was too thick.

Producers did find his British accent appealing, however, and Grant won a part as a sailor in the 10-minute short *Singapore Sue* (1931), for Paramount Pictures. They were pleased with the result and offered him a contract for $450 a week with the condition that he change his name. Remembering his stage role of Cary Lockwood, Grant hoped to use the name as his own. There was already a Lockwood on the studio's payroll, so he was given a list of surnames to choose from and settled on "Grant."

Once retained by the studio, Cary Grant was put to work on *This is the Night* (1932). Listed fifth on the cast list, he plays an Olympic javelin thrower whose wife is involved with a millionaire playboy. Grant was described in movie ads as "the new he-man sensation of Cinemerica!" Unfortunately, he plays as if he were still onstage — overacting to reach the balcony. When Grant first saw the film, he walked out in embarrassment.

Moviegoers looked on his performance more favorably, however, and he was soon cast in a supporting role with Carole Lombard in *Sinners in the Sun* (1932). As a playboy gambler, he is the essence of elegance in his black tie and tails. He also played the lead opposite Nancy Carroll in the forgotten romantic comedy *Hot Saturday* (1932). Only after Mae West selected Grant to be her leading man in *She Done Him Wrong* (1933) did he become one of Paramount's top stars.

Grant (with Charlie Ruggles) in his first feature film, This Is the Night (1932).

His most endearing roles crackle with sexual tension and romantic longing without ever stooping to the obvious.

Grant, a year after his feature debut, was cast in Woman Accused (1933), with John Halliday and Nancy Carroll.

KATHARINE HEPBURN

Hepburn was branded box office poison by motion picture exhibitors in the late thirties. There aren't many stars who could recover from such a devastating assessment, but true to form, Hepburn simply turned her back on Hollywood and headed back to Broadway to produce and star in the comedy smash *The Philadelphia Story*. When the studios inquired about the film rights, Hepburn shrewdly attached herself to the property. With co-stars James Stewart and Cary Grant providing box office insurance, Hepburn made a triumphant return to Hollywood in George Cukor's 1940 film version of the play. That Hepburn orchestrated her comeback came as no surprise to those who knew her. Her trademark ingenuity, integrity, and self-confidence are the very qualities that have made Hepburn an icon.

A dyed-in-the-wool Yankee, the outspoken Hepburn was born May 12, 1907, in Hartford, Connecticut, to a lawyer and a suffragette, both of whom urged their children to speak their minds and take risks. A natural athlete and fierce competitor, Hepburn eventually turned her energies to acting. She appeared in a few plays while attending Bryn Mawr College, then headed to Broadway following her graduation. Her unusual beauty and husky Bryn Mawr accent attracted attention, and soon won her the lead in the Broadway production of *A Warrior's Husband*. Playing an Amazon princess, Hepburn made a spectacular entrance each performance with a 15-foot leap onto the stage.

Always looking for new talent, Hollywood executives came calling, but Hepburn wasn't particularly interested. She felt that theater was her destiny and demanded an outrageous salary. To her surprise, RKO Pictures met her demands, offering her a $1,500-a-week contract contingent on Hepburn passing their standard screen test. She read from *Holiday*, the Philip Barry play she had performed before. That decision turned out to be a wise one. While RKO executive David O. Selznick felt she was unattractive, director George Cukor was so moved by one aspect of her performance — the way she gently set down a glass upon hearing bad news — that he appealed to Selznick to try her in the 1932 film *A Bill of Divorcement*, which starred John Barrymore and Billie Burke. In an effort to tone down Hepburn's severe appearance, Cukor had her cut her hair to chin length and fluff it out to round out her face.

The film's production ran smoothly, though apparently not without incident. As rumor has it, Hepburn had a run-in with John Barrymore, whose glory days as "The Great Profile" were long behind him. An alcoholic with a weakness for young actresses, Barrymore reportedly cornered her and threw off all his clothes,

Hepburn at age fourteen.

Hepburn, opposite David Manners, in her auspicious film debut — A Bill of Divorcement (1932).

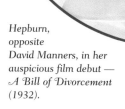

A year after her film debut, Hepburn starred with Douglas Fairbanks Jr. in Morning Glory (1933), a film that earned her the first of four Oscars.

declaring his intention to make love to her. Hepburn escaped and the two returned to the set to play father and daughter under George Cukor's direction.

In this family drama, Hepburn plays Sydney Fairfield, a tireless caretaker for her mentally ill father, played by Barrymore. Sydney ultimately passes up her chance at happiness by refusing to marry her fiancé out of fear that she might inherit her father's mental illness. Hepburn gives a performance that is both strong-willed and vulnerable. Her angular beauty and Yankee sensibility shine through, setting her apart from the soft-faced ingénues of the period.

Selznick was still lukewarm about Hepburn after filming wrapped, but when the movie became a hit, his business sense won out and RKO signed her to a five-year contract. After the first screening, a reviewer for the Hollywood Reporter wrote, "After last night there is a new star on the horizon, and her name is Katharine Hepburn."

In the following year, 1933, she appeared in three highly successful films: *Christopher Strong,* in which she received her first above-the-title billing, playing a young aviatrix; *Little Women,* perfectly cast in the role of Jo; and *Morning Glory,* which earned her the first of her record four Academy Awards.

> **"After last night there is a new star on the horizon, and her name is Katharine Hepburn."**
>
> — *The Hollywood Reporter* on Hepburn's screen debut

LAURENCE OLIVIER

A 1933 MGM publicity shot of Olivier.

Olivier in Too Many Crooks (1930), one of his first film roles.

Greatness was predicted for Laurence Olivier as early as his stage debut at age nine. From the very beginning, he had a theory about acting that he later expressed at the time he was making *Marathon Man* (1976), playing opposite Method-actor Dustin Hoffman. Hoffman had stayed up all night before shooting a torture scene as a way to capture his character's anguish. His efforts did not go unnoticed by Sir Laurence, who is rumored to have quipped, "My dear boy, why not try *acting*?"

Laurence Olivier's unique blend of polished craftsmanship and careful psychological study was not aimed at strict plausibility, but rather precise dramatic effect. Instead of convincing audiences that he was a given character, Olivier's stylized performances were intended to persuade them to suspend their disbelief. His own remark on the subject says it best: "Acting is illusion, as much illusion as magic is, and not so much a matter of being real."

Olivier's first performance, at age nine, as Brutus in a school production of Shakespeare's *Julius Caesar,* bowled over none other than the celebrated stage actress Dame Sybil Thorndike, who predicted that he would go on to have a brilliant career.

The son of a strict Anglican minister and his wife, Olivier was born May 22, 1907, and grew up in Dorking, Surrey, in England. Luckily for the aspiring actor, his father shared his son's love of theater and heartily endorsed Laurence's acting ambitions. With his father's blessing, Olivier continued exploring his passion for the stage at St. Edward's School, an all-boys academy where he was often cast in female parts, in keeping with the custom of the Elizabethan era, when female characters were portrayed by young men. At the age of seventeen he was offered admission to the Central School of Dramatic Art, a prestigious acting college, where he studied under the legendary character actor Claude Rains.

A star pupil, Olivier spent less than a year in London before landing his first paying role in the theater in *The Suliot Officer.* Soon after, he joined the well-regarded Birmingham Repertory, and by 1929 had made a name for himself as an impeccable stage craftsman. Meanwhile, motion pictures were quickly overshadowing the stage, both in the public consciousness and as a lucrative forum for actors.

With stage salaries declining, Olivier turned his attention to film. He made his feature debut in *The Temporary Widow* (1930), a mystery spoof based on the work of German playwright Curt Goetz and filmed in Berlin. Olivier plays Peter Bille, a painter who fabricates his own murder as a publicity stunt. Filming lasted only six weeks, but Olivier gives a competent, if not especially inspired, performance. He hadn't yet adapted his commanding stage presence to the screen, and much of the nuance and subtlety of his performance was lost to the camera's eye.

Nonetheless, Olivier was extremely happy to earn three hundred pounds in such a short time and for much less work than stage productions required. When he was offered a similar amount to star in the comedy short *Too Many Crooks* (1930), Olivier jumped at the chance. This time, his outstanding performance as a wealthy ladies' man is enough to rescue an otherwise forgettable production.

His talent and looks soon grabbed Hollywood's attention. He won the role of Greta Garbo's lover in the historical epic *Queen Christina* (1933), but was abruptly fired when he

and Garbo clashed and she insisted her former co-star John Gilbert get the role. Undaunted, Olivier went back to England where he strung together a series of legendary film and theater performances, most notably in *Fire Over England* (1937), opposite future wife Vivien Leigh. True American-movie stardom followed in 1939, when William Wyler cast him as the brooding Heathcliff in his adaptation of Emily Brontë's *Wuthering Heights* (1939). Olivier received an Academy Award nomination for Best Actor, the first of ten acting nominations that would eventually bring him the prize for his 1948 version of *Hamlet*, which he also produced and directed. It is considered one of the greatest adaptations of Shakespeare ever filmed. By this time his status as the English language's foremost living actor was undisputed. It was a title he would not relinquish until his death in 1989.

> **"Acting is illusion, as much illusion as magic is, and not so much a matter of being real."**
>
> — Laurence Olivier

MICKEY ROONEY

Much like his future co-star and close friend, Judy Garland, Mickey Rooney was born to vaudeville performers who thrust their precocious son onto the stage before he could even assemble a complete sentence. By the age of seven, he had become a star, and by eighteen he had won a special Oscar citing his "significant contribution in bringing to the screen the spirit and personification of youth."

Before all the accolades, he was Joe Yule Jr., born on September 23, 1920, in Brooklyn. His father's philandering broke up both the family and the successful stage act they had become when Rooney was only four, sending the boy and his mother into desperate financial straits. Confident of her son's talents, Nell Yule moved the two of them to California to find him work in the movies.

Rooney and his mother tirelessly visited Hollywood's casting offices in search of film or theater jobs until, finally, the Orange Grove Theater offered him a part in one of its cabaret shows. On opening night, a 20th Century Fox talent scout caught the show and called Yule's mother a few weeks later about a role in an upcoming silent short entitled *Not To Be Trusted*. In his interview with the director, the five-year-old future star claimed to be two. He was following the instructions of his mother, who hoped to make her talented son seem to be even more of a prodigy.

The ruse worked. Rooney was cast in the role of a hard-boiled midget, who poses as a child to infiltrate the home of a rich family and steal their jewels. Working with established comedians Matt Moore and Bud Jamison, he gives a hilarious performance in what would soon become a stock role. In several especially funny scenes, he complains bitterly to his accomplices about the misery of being coddled like a child.

His performance in *Not To Be Trusted* caught the eye of director Alfred Santell, who hired Rooney to reprise his midget role for comic relief in the 1927 feature *Orchids and Ermine*, another silent film. But the young actor's real talent was yet to be discovered. With the advent of the talkies, the world would hear from this new star.

In the role of Mickey McGuire, he played the central character in a series of two-reel talkies based on the popular comic strip Toonerville Folks. With the overwhelming success of the films, he would become known to the world by the name of the character he created, "Mickey." He became so closely associated with the character, which he portrayed in fifty two-reelers, that he had his name legally changed to Mickey McGuire, but finally settled upon Mickey Rooney in 1932, when he made the leap from two-reelers to small roles in feature films.

Rooney's infectious energy and musical talents soon attracted the attention of the major studios. After a hammy turn as Puck in the Warner Brothers all-star adaptation of *A Midsummer Night's Dream* (1935), Rooney moved to MGM, where he befriended Judy Garland. The friends would later team in a series of "barnyard musicals" that propelled both of them to stardom.

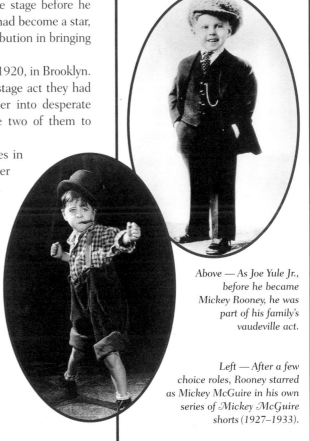

Above — As Joe Yule Jr., before he became Mickey Rooney, he was part of his family's vaudeville act.

Left — After a few choice roles, Rooney starred as Mickey McGuire in his own series of Mickey McGuire shorts (1927–1933).

A scene from The Beast of the City (1932) — one of Rooney's earliest feature films.

JAMES STEWART

Stewart at age eight in a family photo.

> **"If Bess and I had a son, we'd want him to be just like Jimmy Stewart."**
>
> — Harry Truman

In an era when the movies showcased derring-do western heroes and suave, urbane sophisticates, Stewart was a good-natured fellow whose endearing "aw, shucks" persona evoked small-town, all-American virtues. Perhaps because the America of the thirties really did espouse the same value system, Stewart won over audiences who were inherently uncomfortable with the hedonistic mores that had emerged from the infamous Roaring Twenties. At the same time, America's rising urban class was rejecting traditional small-town values, despite the fact that they remained the cornerstones of American culture. Amid the fray, there stood Jimmy Stewart, stuttering his way across the screen.

Norman Rockwell would have found inspiration in Jimmy Stewart's childhood. Born James Maitland Stewart on May 20, 1908 in Indiana, Pennsylvania, to a hardware-store owner and his wife, he grew up in a close, loving family of folks who were regular churchgoers and devoted to music. When Stewart wasn't helping his father at the store, he practiced playing the accordion, which had been a gift from his father.

His skill with the accordion earned Stewart a spot with the Triangle Players at Princeton University, where he was studying architecture. He graduated in 1932 and headed to Cape Cod to spend the summer with the University Players in Falmouth, Massachusetts. Princeton classmate and future Broadway director Joshua Logan had talked Stewart into joining the troupe, where he befriended Henry Fonda and Margaret Sullavan and honed his acting skills.

With little more than his accordion, Stewart threw caution to the wind and moved to New York City, where he and roommate Fonda earned money by hosting the Thursday Night Beer Club. Fonda cooked up hobo steaks and Stewart sang and played the accordion to pay the rent. Meanwhile, they both auditioned tirelessly.

Stewart had more luck than Fonda in those early days, though he was initially turned down for the part of Sergeant O'Hara in the Broadway production of *Yellow Jack* because producers felt his Irish brogue was not convincing. He sought out an Irish friend for a crash course in the dialect and ultimately landed the role. Until this time, Stewart had yet to consider acting to be a realistic ambition, but the cast of *Yellow Jack,* which consisted of true professionals, taught him to take his craft seriously. Although his performance won critical acclaim, it wasn't enough to save the production from going under. When it closed after ten weeks, Stewart's friend Hedda Hopper, herself just an aspiring actress at the time, helped him get a screen test at MGM. He impressed studio executives enough to earn a long-term contract for $350 a week and a trip to Hollywood.

After an uncredited role in the comedy short *Art Trouble* (1934), he made his feature-film debut with a small role in the 1935 film *The Murder Man,* starring Spencer Tracy. Tracy plays an ace reporter whose scoop leads to the arrest and conviction of a murder suspect, who may in fact be innocent. As Shorty, Stewart plays a cub reporter whose ill-fitting nickname adds a welcome bit of levity to the rather grim proceedings. Despite good reviews, the movie never quite became a hit.

If *The Murder Man* did little to boost Tracy's Hollywood profile, it did even less for Stewart, who wasn't considered leading-man material. He next played a supporting role in the MGM operetta, *Rose-Marie* (1936), as Jeanette MacDonald's younger brother.

Stewart's powerful performance as a fugitive hiding out in the Canadian wilderness earned him a leading role in Universal's *Next Time We Love* (1936), with a little help from an old friend. Margaret Sullavan, an old friend from their Cape Cod theater days, lobbied Universal executives to cast Stewart to play her husband in this romantic melodrama about a young couple juggling marriage and career. Reviews hailed Stewart as a promising newcomer. Stardom would follow three years later with *Mr. Smith Goes to Washington*, which brought him his first Oscar nomination.

Stewart (opposite Margaret Sullavan) as Christopher Tyler in Next Time We Love (1936), his first substantial role.

SHIRLEY TEMPLE

To cinematic audiences of the era she represented a sunny, unspoiled innocence, a momentary relief from the hardships wrought of the Depression.

Temple at the age of two — four years before she became a star.

Temple debuted in Baby Burlesk shorts in 1932.

The number one box office star in the country by the time she was eight years old, Shirley Temple almost single-handedly kept 20th Century Fox afloat during the thirties. She represented a sunny, unspoiled innocence, a momentary relief from the hardship of the Depression. Whether she was tap-dancing with Bill "Bojangles" Robinson or facing off against her nemesis, the spoiled Jane Withers, Temple's energy and charm, her ability to elicit laughter and tears — often at the very same time — gave audiences a much needed escape from their worries and provided hope for a better future.

The youngest of three children and the only girl, Shirley Temple was born on April 23, 1928, in Santa Monica, California. From infancy, her mother began grooming Shirley for stardom. She enrolled the toddler in Mrs. Meglin's Dance Studio, which was frequented by talent scouts from the Poverty Row studio, Educational Films Corporation. That studio was currently making a series of two-reelers called *Baby Burlesk,* which featured toddlers dressed as adults and mouthing hard-boiled dialogue.

Temple's energy and confidence bowled over the scouts, who cast her in the short *War Babies* (1932), part of the Baby Burlesk series. In her film debut, she plays Charmaine, a saloon waitress who flirts with the patrons, two-fisted milk-drinkers every last one, for tips — lollipops. She remains unruffled, even when the diaper-wearing patrons begin to get rowdy. Eventually the white-diapered hero comes to her rescue. As always, her performance is pricelessly cute.

Temple made only a few more *Baby Burlesk* shorts before moving on to bit parts in major studio productions. In 1932, she made her first feature, *Red-Haired Alibi,* one of several that year, all of the B-movie variety, but thirties audiences were beginning to show a real affection for Temple and other child actors. Realizing the potential, Gertrude Temple began to carefully mold Shirley into a fine young actress. Each night, a special ritual consisted of coiling locks of young Shirley's hair into exactly 52 uniform curls.

In 1933 Temple starred in four films, but it wasn't until *Stand Up and Cheer* (1934) that she began to steal scenes from her fellow actors. She soon became a fixture on the nation's movie theater marquees. *Stand Up and Cheer* elevated the young actress from bit player to genuine child star. Not long after its release, 20th Century Fox signed her to a contract. Doubting the lasting power of her juvenile charm they cast her in no fewer than twelve movies that year. She went on to star in *Little Miss Marker,* opposite Adolphe Menjou, and *Bright Eyes* (1934), which features her performing her signature song, "On the Good Ship Lollipop." At year's end, Temple was awarded a special Academy Award for her "outstanding contribution to screen entertainment." Her fame would soon eclipse that of more established stars and propel her to the top of the box office for the rest of the decade.

SPENCER TRACY

He wasn't Hollywood's typical leading man. He had neither the urbane sophistication of Cary Grant nor the rugged glamour of Clark Gable, but what Spencer Tracy did bring to his performances — unquestioned integrity and innate sensibility — made it easy for him to establish a lasting bond with audiences. Unlike Grant or Gable, he was leery about chasing stardom. As his longtime companion Katharine Hepburn once said, "I think Spencer always thought acting was a rather silly way for a man to make a living."

Spencer Bonaventure Tracy was born on April 5, 1900, in Milwaukee, to Irish-Catholic parents. He was expelled from no fewer than a dozen grade schools before turning things around at the Marquette Academy, where his grades and attitude improved. In fact, until joining the Navy at the onset of World War I, Tracy had ambitions to become a doctor or a priest. When he returned from the war, however, as a student at Ripon College, he discovered acting to be his true calling.

Reluctantly bankrolled by his father, Tracy went on to attend the New York Academy of Dramatic Arts, where he roomed with fellow Marquette alumnus Pat O'Brien. A series of menial jobs — bellman, janitor, door-to-door salesman — kept him just barely afloat while he went from audition to audition, furiously pursuing that elusive first paying gig. When he finally did land a paying job in the theater, it was a non-speaking role as a robot in the play *R.U.R.* for the grand sum of $15 per week. Within a few weeks, he earned a promotion to a small speaking part and a raise to $25 per week.

In 1929, with his career still falling way short of his expectations, he resolved to give his ambition of acting for a living just one last shot before packing it all in and heading home. The final audition was for the lead in a Broadway play aptly titled *The Last Mile,* and after seven long years of chasing his dream, his persistence was finally rewarded. He won the role, and then won critical raves for his performance as Killer Meers in the tense prison drama. The play received added publicity because of the fact that the Auburn Prison riot, an event that made news around the country, occurred just before *The Last Mile* opened.

Among the many to notice Tracy's riveting performance was John Ford, who was casting the lead role in the film he was about to direct based on the Auburn Prison riots, *Up the River* (1930). Despite a screen test that was poorly received by the executives at 20th Century Fox, Ford hired Tracy to play alongside Humphrey Bogart (acting in only his second feature film) in the film that marks a milestone in both their careers. Sadly, it was the last time the trio of film greats — Tracy, Ford, and Bogart — was ever to collaborate.

Tracy's understated, less-is-more approach to acting continued to impress critics and audiences alike. By the end of the thirties, he was one of Hollywood's most honored stars, winning back-to-back Best Actor Oscars in 1937 and 1938 for *Captains Courageous* and *Boys Town*.

> **"Spencer always thought acting was a rather silly way for a grown man to make a living."**
>
> — Katharine Hepburn

Tracy became the first actor to win two successive Oscars — for 1937's Captains Courageous *(above) and* Boys Town *(1938).*

JOHN WAYNE

Before he was a movie star, he was a football star at USC (circa 1926).

Before Wayne (left) broke out in Stagecoach (1939), he appeared in a number of minor films and shorts, including this one, Shadow of the Eagle (1932).

Facing page —
Wayne (left), in
his first leading role,
The Big Trail (1930).

John Wayne, Hollywood's favorite cowboy of the forties and fifties, was born Marion Michael Morrison on May 26, 1907, in Winterset, Iowa. His father was a pharmacist and his mother a housewife. The future star of westerns developed an early aversion to horses riding one to school every day, but the family later moved to California, where Wayne worked odd jobs, selling newspapers and delivering medicine for his father. His beloved Airedale Terrier named Duke, was the source of the moniker he would be identified with for decades to come.

A good student and athlete, Wayne was named an alternate candidate to attend the U.S. Naval Academy in Annapolis. But when the appointment went to another applicant, he instead accepted a scholarship to play football at the University of Southern California in 1925. His coach at USC found a summer job for Duke as a prop boy at 20th Century Fox, where he met and befriended director John Ford, who became a lifelong friend and mentor.

When Wayne left USC, he returned to filmmaking as a laborer behind the scenes before seeking acting roles in earnest. John Ford used him in several movies as an uncredited extra, and he picked up a supporting role as a composer in the early musical *Words and Music* (1929), where he is billed as "Duke Morrison."

Wayne's first leading role came in Raoul Walsh's epic western *The Big Trail* (1930), which was shot in both 35mm and the widescreen 70mm process called Fox Grandeur. Walsh provided invaluable career advice to the screen novice. Not only did he suggest that Duke Morrison change his name to the tougher-sounding "John Wayne," but he also taught him how to look and feel comfortable on a horse — a skill that would be of inestimable value in years to come.

In *The Big Trail*, Wayne plays Breck Coleman, a mountaineer who leads a wagon train of pioneers out west. The settlers contend with Indian attacks, storms, overflowing rivers, and a traitor in their company who is plotting to betray them for financial gain. In a demanding role that would have challenged even a much more experienced actor, Wayne repays every ounce of Walsh's faith in him. Not just a convincing action hero, Wayne demonstrates a confidence and ease in his love scenes with Marguerite Churchill, who plays a pretty settler. It was a star-making performance, and Wayne seemed destined to take his place alongside such cowboy luminaries as Tom Mix and William Boyd.

Unfortunately, *The Big Trail* was a financial and critical failure. Most Depression-era movie theaters were ill-equipped to show the Fox Grandeur 70mm version and had to settle for the far inferior 35mm print. After losing much money on *The Big Trail,* the executives at 20th Century pinned the blame on Wayne and terminated his contract. Sentenced to starring in low-budget Poverty Row westerns for the rest of the decade, Wayne finally became a star when John Ford cast him as the Ringo Kid in the 1939 western classic *Stagecoach.*

OL' SONG AND DANCE

The primitive recording technology of the late twenties and early thirties may have ruined many a silent film star's career, but it also gave birth to the musical. Except for Rin Tin Tin, it seemed almost every star was forced to warble a tune or dance, regardless of their musical talents; listen to Jimmy Stewart's quavery rendition of Cole Porter's "Easy to Love" in *Born to Dance* (1936) and you'll understand why he stuck to comedy and drama. The following performers became stars in thirties-era musicals that continue to entertain music lovers and connoisseurs of camp.

Jeanette MacDonald and **Nelson Eddy** were known as "America's Sweethearts" in the mid-thirties. Eddy sang in the church choir before winning a competition to earn a place in the Philadelphia Civic Opera. MGM signed him to a contract and gave him a part in two 1933 musicals, *Dancing Lady* and *Broadway to Hollywood*. MacDonald worked as a chorus girl on Broadway before Paramount lured her to Hollywood for the lead in *The Love Parade* in 1929. In 1935, MGM put them together in *Naughty Marietta*, and their popularity soared. The pair appeared in more than a half dozen films before one of Hollywood's best-loved pairings split in 1942.

Betty Grable was a talented singer and dancer who landed her first movie role as a bit player when she was just fourteen in the 1930 film, *Let's Go Places*. She worked steadily through the thirties, usually in second leads, until 1939's *Million Dollar Legs*, which lifted her from the ranks of contract player to full-fledged star. Her perfectly sculpted dancer's legs, insured by Lloyd's of London, became all the rage in the 1940s, when she finally became a big star and every American GI's favorite pin-up.

Ginger Rogers, born Virginia Katherine McMath, will forever be linked with the fleet-footed Fred Astaire, but Rogers was an accomplished singer, dancer, and actor in her own right well before that partnership was formed. Pushed towards stardom by a domineering mother, Rogers began her acting career as a child, singing and dancing on the vaudeville circuit before landing her first movie role in the 1929 short, *A Night in a Dormitory*. After a few supporting roles, Rogers teamed up with Astaire in RKO's *Flying Down to Rio* (1933) and became an acknowledged star in their breezy follow-up, *The Gay Divorcee* (1934).

Jeanette MacDonald

Nelson Eddy

Ginger Rogers

Betty Grable

GANGSTERS OF THE DEPRESSION ERA

The gangster film has always been a successful Hollywood genre. From the days of the first *Scarface* (1932), public enemies and racketeers have long been the subject of big-screen adulation and condemnation. Many actors carved out long careers portraying these ruthless hoods on the screen. Below are just some of the actors who rose to stardom playing gangsters in the hard-hitting, Depression-era crime dramas.

"Bogie" (Humphrey Bogart)   *James Cagney*   *Paul Muni*   *George Raft*   *Edward G. Robertson*

Humphrey Bogart, the toughest of the tough guys, was actually born with a silver spoon in his mouth to a well established New York family. He made his name playing vicious killers, including Duke Mantee in *The Petrified Forest* (1936). Other tough guy roles were in *Dead End* (1937), *Angels with Dirty Faces* (1938), *The Roaring Twenties* (1939), and others.

James Cagney's acting talent eventually led him to Broadway and Hollywood. He made his big-screen debut in *Sinner's Holiday* (1930), in which he reprises his role from the hit Broadway play. A year later, Cagney was cast as a prohibition gangster in the successful film *The Public Enemy* (1931). His stellar performance in that film led to many similar roles, including gangster roles in the critically acclaimed films *Angels with Dirty Faces* (1938) and *White Heat* (1949).

Paul Muni was born Muni Weisenfreund in Austria in 1895 to parents who soon left their homeland to act in the Yiddish theaters of New York's Lower East Side. After playing character roles in the Yiddish theater, Muni made his Broadway debut in the 1926 drama, *We Americans.* He made his film debut in *The Valiant* (1929), playing a drifter who accidentally kills the star witness to a crime. Stardom came in 1932, when Muni played the title role in Howard Hawks's ultra-violent crime drama, *Scarface,* a thinly disguised portrayal of the rise and fall of Chicago gangster Al Capone.

George Raft became an overnight screen sensation playing a small-time, coin-flipping hood in *Scarface* (1932). Born and raised in New York's Hell's Kitchen, Raft first tried prize-fighting and then became a dancer on Broadway and in Prohibition-era nightclubs, where he got to know some of the biggest racketeers in the city. From his movie debut in *Queen of the Nightclubs* (1929), he established himself as a movie gangster.

Edward G. Robinson, born Emmanuel Goldenberg, made a career out of portraying gangsters. After graduating from the American Academy of Dramatic Arts, Goldenberg, who had by then changed his name to Edward G. Robinson, began acting on the stage, eventually landing on Broadway, where he enjoyed some success. Early in his career, he made a brief appearance in the 1923 silent film *The Bright Shawl,* but Robinson's film breakthrough would come in 1930's *Little Caesar* as gangster heavy Rico Bandello, whose dying words, "Is this the end of Rico?" have entered our pop culture vernacular.

OTHER STARS OF THE PERIOD

Ingrid Bergman   Marlene Dietrich   William Holden

Ingrid Bergman, forever immortalized by her part as Ilsa in *Casablanca* (1942), was born in Stockholm, Sweden, in 1915. Orphaned at an early age, Bergman was raised by relatives and graduated from the Royal Dramatic Theater School. In 1932, she landed a bit part in the Swedish film, *Landskamp*. A tiny role in the comedy *Munkbrovregen* (1934) led to better roles, including the lead in the romance, *Intermezzo* (1936). The fresh-faced, radiantly beautiful actress impressed David O. Selznick, who brought her to America to star in a Hollywood remake of *Intermezzo* opposite Leslie Howard in 1939. She became one of the top stars of the forties, winning her first of three Oscars in 1944 for *Gaslight*.

Marlene Dietrich was born Maria Magdalene Dietrich in Berlin, Germany, in 1901. She began her career on the German stage before landing several roles in the movies, the first of which was a small part in the silent film *Der Kleine Napoleon* (1923). Her big break came as Lola Lola, the sexy cabaret singer who ruins a college professor in the 1930 German film, *The Blue Angel*. After that success, she arrived in Hollywood with much fanfare and enjoyed a very successful film and cabaret career in the United States.

William Holden, born William Franklin Beedle Jr., to an industrial chemist father and a teacher mother, was spotted by a Hollywood talent scout while he was attending Pasadena Junior College. At the age of twenty, he made his big-screen debut as an extra in the 1938 film, *Prison Farm*. His breakthrough role came the following year with the lead in Clifford Odets's boxing drama, *Golden Boy* (1939). Hollywood lore has it that Holden would have lost the role if not for the efforts of veteran co-star Barbara Stanwyck, who worked with the novice to calm his nerves. His performance as the violinist turned prizefighter established Holden as a talent to watch.

Bob Hope   Vivien Leigh   Mae West

Bob Hope immigrated to the United States from England as a child and became a star comic on the vaudeville circuit of the twenties. The wisecracking stand-up with the seemingly inexhaustible supply of one-liners — many of them ad-libbed — made his film debut in the two-reel short, *Going Spanish* (1934). A Poverty Row quickie production, *Going Spanish* was Hope's first and last two-reeler for Educational Films. His starring role on radio's *Pepsodent Show* led to his first role in a major studio release, Paramount's *The Big Broadcast of 1938,* in which he shares the screen with comic greats W.C. Fields and Martha Raye. He would later team up with Bing Crosby for the popular "road" series.

Vivien Leigh, née Hartley, was born in India and later educated at an English convent school. She made her big-screen debut in the 1935 film, *The Village Squire.* The petite, classically lovely Leigh was a star in the making whose performance in the costume drama, *Fire Over England* (1937), impressed David O. Selznick. He gave her the much-coveted role of the conniving Southern belle Scarlett O'Hara in *Gone With the Wind* (1939). Leigh's performance earned her an Academy Award, the first of two Oscars she would win during her career.

Mae West, the queen of the one-liner, started acting on stage at the age of five. The precocious child soon moved on to burlesque, where she became known as the "Baby Vamp," before perfecting her shimmy in a variety of vaudeville shows. She eventually graduated to Broadway, where her 1926 play, *Sex* — which she wrote, produced, and directed — was shut down by the police. In 1932 the buxom blonde made a scene-stealing debut in *Night After Night.* She followed this with the hugely popular *She Done Him Wrong* (1933), an adaptation of her stage play, *Diamond Lil.*

1940-1949

Walt Disney's
Pinocchio (1940).

World War I is the
subject of one of the
first patriotic theme
movies of the World
War II years — *For Me
and My Gal* (1942),
starring George Murphy, Judy
Garland, and Gene Kelly (in his
first movie role).

*Five bucks buys you a bomb in
Blondie for Victory (1942).*

WAR AND PEACE

A merica's entry into World War II had an immediate impact on the film industry. Following the declaration of war against Japan, the U.S. Government worked with Hollywood to establish the Bureau of Motion Picture Affairs. The Bureau's purpose was to coordinate the production of entertainment with patriotic, morale-boosting themes and messages. At first, Hollywood responded with films like *Blondie for Victory* and *The Devil with Hitler,* both released in 1942. These films soon gave way to the patriotic heroics of John Wayne, who seemed capable of defeating the enemy single-handedly in such films as *The Flying Tigers* (1942) or 1944's *The Fighting Seabees.* More propaganda than art, these films were extremely popular with wartime audiences.

As the war continued and casualties mounted, the war films became more realistic and veteran filmmakers Frank Capra, John Ford, and William Wyler were enlisted to make documentaries for the armed forces. Many stars, such as Clark Gable, Jimmy Stewart, and Robert Montgomery enlisted in the armed services. With such marquee favorites missing in action from the nation's screens, female stars like Betty Grable, Ingrid Bergman, and Greer Garson stepped into the limelight.

Not all male stars enlisted. Bogart, Cagney, Tracy, and Bing Crosby continued as headliners, while newcomers such as Gregory Peck and Gene Kelly made stellar debuts.

Feature animation brought lush color and wholesome entertainment to wartime audiences. Following up on the 1937 success of his feature-length cartoon *Snow White and the Seven Dwarfs,* Walt Disney produced the classic cartoons *Pinocchio* (1940), *Fantasia* (1940), *Dumbo* (1941), and *Bambi* (1942).

Not to be outdone, Warner Brothers introduced the irrepressible Bugs Bunny in 1940, and Daffy Duck and Elmer Fudd soon joined him. That same year, Walter Lantz unveiled his manic creation, Woody Woodpecker.

The end of the war saw theater attendance hit an all-time high. Returning soldiers flocked to the movies. Large-scale, extravagant musicals returned, and MGM released such classics as *Anchors Aweigh* (1945), *The Pirate* (1948), and *On the Town* (1949), the last of which paired Gene Kelly with singing sensation Frank Sinatra. Judy Garland became a full-fledged adult star in the MGM musicals *Meet Me in St. Louis* (1944) and *The Harvey Girls* (1946), while veteran Fred Astaire continued to astonish audiences with his inventive choreography.

Another genre that took off after the war was the western. John Ford directed such classics as *My Darling Clementine* (1946) and *Fort Apache* (1948), the latter starring John Wayne. Wayne also starred with newcomer Montgomery Clift in Howard Hawks's *Red River* (1948).

Post-war audiences also flocked to much more serious and topical films. Elia Kazan's *Gentleman's Agreement* (1947) dramatizes anti-Semitism in contemporary America; Billy Wilder depicts a writer's harrowing descent into alcoholism in *The Lost Weekend* (1945); and Anatole Litvak's *The Snake Pit* (1948) dramatizes a woman's nightmarish confinement to a mental institution.

War's end also brought heightened fears of a Communist presence in the United States. The Cold War panic sweeping the country hit Hollywood in 1947, when the House Un-American Activities Committee (HUAC) opened hearings to investigate alleged Communist influence in films. More than 100 witnesses, including some of Hollywood's most famous stars, were called before the committee to answer questions about their own or their colleagues' alleged Communist affiliations. On November 24, 1947, a group of eight screenwriters and two directors, the famous "Hollywood Ten," were sentenced to serve prison terms for refusing to testify. The studios quickly banded together and issued a statement declaring that they would not hire any talent with Communist affiliations.

The result was catastrophic. Hundreds were fired from the studios and many talented writers, directors, and actors were ruined on the basis of hearsay or the flimsiest evidence. It took years, in some cases decades, for some to regain their careers, and many never did.

Hal Roach's The Devil with Hitler (1942).

Hollywood dove into the War effort—Gregory Peck pitching war bonds in 1943.

Former big band singer Doris Day debuted in Romance on the High Seas (1948), a post-war musical.

DORIS DAY

> **"I knew Doris Day before she was a virgin."**
>
> — Oscar Levant

Day in 1940, when she was a singer for Les Brown and his orchestra.

Day with
Jack Carson (left)
and Fortunio Bonanova in her screen debut in *Romance on the High Seas* (1948).

Hollywood wit Oscar Levant once quipped, "I knew Doris Day before she was a virgin." Her innocent, even prudish screen persona, most notably seen in the hit films she made with Rock Hudson, was established in her first film, *Romance on the High Seas* (1948), and ultimately led to her being typecast and unfairly labeled as Hollywood's goody-goody girl.

Strange as it may sound, a car accident provided the unlikely impetus for Day's singing career. Born Doris Mary Ann von Kappelhoff on April 3, 1924 in Cincinnati, Ohio, as a young girl she aspired to dance professionally. Injured in a car accident and unable to pursue this ambition, Day began singing along with the radio during her lengthy convalescence. She made a minor splash singing "Day After Day" on a student-run radio show, and shortly after looked to singing as her professional destiny. Just eighteen months after the accident, Day beat out over 200 other girls to sing with Barney Rapp's band. All that remained was choosing a more marquee-friendly name. Rapp suggested "Day," after her radio debut song. At age sixteen, Doris left both the von Kappelhoff name and Cincinnati behind to go on the road with Rapp's band.

Her singing career took off and Day sang with several well-known bands over the next few years, including those of Jimmy James, Bob Crosby, and Les Brown. With Brown's Band, she entertained troops in Europe, and in 1944 they recorded "Sentimental Journey," which became both the servicemen's theme song and Day's first million-record-selling hit.

Unfortunately, success took a toll on her personal life, and by 1947 Day had been married and divorced twice. Ready to leave Hollywood and its memories behind, she initially resisted her agent's advice to stay and screen test for a role in the upcoming Warner Brothers movie *Romance on the High Seas*. The film's director, Michael Curtiz, had already tested 100 women, including Judy Garland and Betty Hutton, but none of them seemed right for the part of singer Georgia Garrett. That Day had never professionally acted before didn't faze her agent, who finally persuaded her to stay and meet with Curtiz.

At her audition, Day was less than enthusiastic, explaining that she was on her way to New York. She admitted that she had no experience and wasn't even sure that she wanted to act. She reluctantly agreed to sing, but a few bars into "Embraceable You," the romantic lyrics saddened her and she began to cry. To her surprise, Curtiz was impressed by her sensitivity, telling her that sometimes he hired women who weren't trained actresses because their emotions were straight from the heart. He hired her the next day.

In the film, Day plays a lonely nightclub singer who dreams of traveling to faraway places. When she meets a woman who suspects that her husband is cheating, Day agrees to take her place on a cruise so the wife can stay home and spy on him. In a time-honored Hollywood contrivance, the woman's husband also suspects that she's been unfaithful and hires a private detective to take *his* place on the ship. In this sentimental, breezy musical comedy of mistaken identity, the singer and the private detective naturally fall in love.

A hit with audiences, *Romance on the High Seas* was a double triumph for Day. In addition to racking up another million-selling hit record with the film's song, "It's Magic," she also became a movie star, a position she would occupy until her retirement from the screen in 1968.

KIRK DOUGLAS

Kirk Douglas was born Issur Danielovitch into dire poverty on December 9, 1916 in Amsterdam, New York. From an early age he sought ways to distinguish himself from his peers. His first opportunity came through athletics. In high school, Douglas was a fine all-around athlete, winning a wrestling scholarship to St. Lawrence University. Later, his athletic ability would contribute a defining element to his stardom — the emotional intensity and the physicality he would bring to the heroic role he played in *Spartacus* (1960).

At St. Lawrence, Douglas turned his determination and deeply ingrained work ethic to acting. The results won him favorable notice in several student-sponsored theatrical performances, and these eventually led to a second scholarship – to the famed Academy of Dramatic Arts in New York.

Before long, Douglas had earned himself several small parts in Broadway productions, but this promising start was interrupted when World War II broke out. He entered the Navy in 1942, where he served as a communications officer. Upon his return to New York, Douglas won the role of a ghost soldier in a play called *The Wind Is Ninety*. It was his first major role on Broadway and the buzz from critics was strong enough to spark some interest in Hollywood.

In 1946, Lauren Bacall, a former classmate from the Academy of Dramatic Arts, was at the peak of her fame, fresh off a star-making performance in *To Have and Have Not* (1944) and her marriage to co-star Humphrey Bogart. When she read Douglas's notices for *The Wind Is Ninety,* she persuaded producer Hal Wallis to give him a screen test for an upcoming film noir project called *The Strange Love of Martha Ivers.*

When Douglas arrived in Hollywood to meet Wallis, he carried himself with a smooth self-assurance. In fact, one director commented that Douglas "acted like a star even when he was a nobody." Wallis was impressed and offered him the part of Walter O'Neil, a hard-drinking district attorney and husband to Barbara Stanwyck's title character. Played by another actor, Douglas's character might have served simply as a weak foil to Stanwyck's cunning femme fatale. But even in his first role, Douglas displayed a talent for uncovering the depth in an obviously villainous character. When Martha Ivers's childhood love, played by Van Heflin, mysteriously returns to town, O'Neil stops at nothing to drive him away. At the same time, the vulnerability and unrequited love that drives him is apparent to the audience.

A critical and commercial success, *The Strange Love of Martha Ivers* was nominated for a Best Original Motion Picture Story Oscar. Douglas received great reviews for his performance, though he would have to wait three years before achieving marquee billing and an Oscar nomination for his performance as Midge Kelly in *Champion* (1949).

> **When Douglas arrived in Hollywood to meet producer Hal Wallis, he carried himself with a smooth self-assurance.**

Douglas opposite Barbara Stanwyck in his motion picture debut, The Strange Love of Martha Ivers (1946).

Douglas, as another "son of a bitch," was nominated for an Oscar for his portrayal of Michael "Midge" Kelly in Champion (1949).

GENE KELLY

A twenty-year-old Kelly in his college graduation photo.

Gene Kelly's arrival in Hollywood in 1942 marks the end of an era. Movie audiences were used to dance fare featuring exuberant kids like Mickey Rooney and Judy Garland or aristocrats like Fred Astaire and Ginger Rogers elegantly prancing across ornate sets. Then, along came a dancer whose performances included stunning leaps across construction sets, gleeful splashes in the rain, and skirt-chasing in a sailor suit on the town with Frank Sinatra. Gene Kelly, the antithesis of the sophisticated Fred Astaire, was an exuberant athlete whose acrobatic, daring choreography made him one of the top movie musical stars of the forties and fifties.

The third of five children, Eugene Curran Kelly was born August 23, 1912 in Pittsburgh and began taking dance lessons soon after taking his first wobbly steps. By the time he was eight, Gene and his siblings were performing as "The Five Kellys" at local amateur nights. Although Kelly preferred baseball, his mother wouldn't allow him to abandon the dance training that would one day lead to stardom.

After high school Kelly studied economics at the University of Pittsburgh. To support himself, he carried a variety of jobs. He dug ditches and worked as a soda jerk, but constantly found himself turning back to dancing. What had been a means of placating his mother had evolved into a genuine passion. In 1932 he started The Gene Kelly Studio of the Dance in Pittsburgh and Johnstown. It became a family business, with his mother serving as manager, his father as bookkeeper, and the Kelly children as teachers. He taught part-time during his senior year in college and then devoted his attention full-time to the business when he graduated.

By 1937, teaching dance to locals had lost its appeal for Kelly, who was anxious to make the professional leap to Broadway. He received an offer to choreograph a number in a Broadway show, only to learn upon his arrival in New York that he was needed only as a dancer. Kelly declined the offer and returned to Pittsburgh for another year of teaching. In 1938 he returned to Broadway to debut in *Leave it to Me* with newcomer Mary Martin, who became the new darling of Broadway musicals. Kelly's moment in the spotlight came later with his role as Harry the Hoofer in *The Time of Your Life*. His performance won him the lead in Rodgers and Hart's musical *Pal Joey*, a critical and commercial success that ran for 270 performances and won Kelly a movie contract with David O. Selznick.

Unfortunately, Selznick didn't appear to have any specific roles in mind. After five months, he sold Kelly's contract to MGM, who immediately cast him opposite Judy Garland in Busby Berkeley's *For Me and My Gal* (1942). Kelly played Harry Palmer, a

Kelly, with co-star Judy Garland, in For Me and My Gal *(1942) — his feature-film debut.*

vaudeville star who longs to headline at New York's Palace Theater. At the onset of World War I, he deliberately injures his hand to avoid the draft. Disgusted with his cowardice, Harry's partners Jo and Jimmy leave to entertain the troops in France. Guilt-ridden,

Harry ultimately enlists and comes home a war hero. With Jo (Judy Garland) at his side, Harry finally gets the chance to headline at the Palace Theater — the film's cheerful musical finale.

Kelly's brash charm, pleasant singing and athletic dancing in the unabashedly patriotic musical were a huge hit with wartime audiences. Over the next few years, MGM and Kelly made some of the finest musicals of all time, including *On The Town* (1949), *An American in Paris* (1951), and *Singin' in the Rain* (1952).

In 1985, he received The American Film Institute's Lifetime Achievement Award. Director and choreographer Stanley Donen summed up Kelly's career: "Gene was among the wonders of the twentieth century."

"Gene was among the wonders of the twentieth century."

— Stanley Donen

GREGORY PECK

Born on April 5, 1916 in La Jolla, California, Gregory Peck was raised by his grandmother following the divorce of his parents when he was five years old — an event that was to leave emotional scars for years to come. While his family situation caused him anxiety, he found much-needed domestic stability under his grandmother's steady care. As a teenager, Peck drove a truck to earn money for college, enrolling at the University of California at Berkeley with the plan to study medicine. Soon after arriving, the tall, handsome Peck was recruited by the university's drama director for a role in a small student production. Just this small taste of theatrical achievement convinced him to head for New York upon graduation to study acting at the Neighborhood Playhouse with theatrical pioneer Sanford Meisner. In 1942, he made his Broadway debut with a small role in the drama *The Morning Star.*

Peck's performance caught the attention of legendary producer David O. Selznick, and he was soon invited to Hollywood for a screen test. The prospect of higher pay and wider audiences, thrilled him but the screen test was not well received. While Selznick conceded that he "may be a fine legitimate actor," he ultimately threw up his hands: "I don't see what we could do with Gregory Peck."

Disappointed but not disheartened, Peck decided to remain in Hollywood, where he found stage work in *The Willow and I.* Meanwhile, he met and became engaged to a successful young actress named Tamara Toumanova. The engagement didn't last, but it did prove crucial in the launch of Peck's movie career. In 1943, Toumanova was cast as the female lead in *Days of Glory,* a bleak war film. The plot centers on an attractive ballerina who joins a stranded group of guerrillas trying desperately to fend off the Nazi invasion of the USSR. When director Jacques Tourneur needed a male lead to play the brave guerrilla commander, Toumanova suggested her fiancé. After viewing the young actor's screen test, Tourneur agreed to invite him for a reading. Peck's ability to project heroic earnestness won him the lead role of Vladimir.

The onscreen chemistry between Peck's Vladimir and Toumanova's Nina is one of the film's few strong points. Otherwise, the overwrought sentimentality slows the pace of the film. Peck maintains his dignity throughout, despite the preachy dialogue. Though the film opened to mediocre reviews, critics singled out Peck's brilliant performance. World War II had left Hollywood short of leading men, so Peck's impressive debut attracted numerous offers. In 1944, Peck appeared in the 20th Century Fox production *Keys of the Kingdom,* which cast him as a long-suffering missionary in China. The next year he had his breakthrough hit in MGM's *The Valley of Decision,* a story of inter-class romance. Alfred Hitchcock also cast him as the amnesiac lead in the psychological thriller *Spellbound* (1945). Even Selznick, who had initially rejected Peck, hired him to star in the expensive western *Duel in the Sun* (1946). Like the rest of Hollywood, Selznick had finally figured out what to do with Gregory Peck.

Peck in an early family photo.

Peck (opposite Maria Palmer), in his screen debut as Vladimir in Days of Glory (1944).

ELIZABETH TAYLOR

"Her eyes are too old. She doesn't have the face of a kid."

— casting director Dan Kelly on young Taylor's screen prospects.

Taylor in her first feature film, Lassie Come Home (1943) — with Nigel Bruce.

She is the woman who famously told MGM's Louis B. Mayer to "go to hell" when she was a teenage contract player in the forties. It was a measure of her already formidable power that Mayer displayed no wrath and the incident did not damage her career. Since her film debut in 1942, Elizabeth Taylor has won two Academy Awards and five nominations. Often cast as a tempestuous, willful beauty, she was the first actress to earn one million dollars for a film — the 1963 historical epic *Cleopatra.*

The violet-eyed, raven-haired daughter of American expatriates was born on February 27, 1932 in London, England. Originally from St. Louis, Taylor's parents came to London to run an art gallery. When World War II appeared inevitable, the Taylors left London to settle in Los Angeles in 1939.

A former actress, Taylor's mother was determined to make her beautiful daughter a star. She met the chairman of Universal Studios, J. Cheever Cowdin and his wife at the family gallery and invited the couple home. Always on the lookout for new talent, Cowdin signed young Elizabeth to a six-month renewable contract at $100 a week. Shortly thereafter, the nine-year-old actress made her screen debut in the 1942 short film *There's One Born Every Minute* as a bratty little girl who delights in shooting rubber bands at adults and cutting up with her co-star, Carl "Alfalfa" Switzer of *Our Gang* fame. When the short attracted scant attention, Universal dismissed Taylor. Ironically, the studio's casting director, Dan Kelly, underestimated the feature that would become Taylor's claim-to-fame when she made the transition from child actor to adult actress. "Her eyes are too old," he complained at the time. "She doesn't have the face of a kid."

Parental connections brought Taylor a second chance at screen stardom in 1943, this time because of her father's friendship with MGM producer Samuel Marx. The studio was frantically searching for a young girl to star with Roddy McDowall in *Lassie Come Home,* which was already in production. Taylor beat out five other actresses for the role of Priscilla, a wealthy landowner's granddaughter who briefly cares for Lassie in World War I-era Yorkshire, England.

Even though Lassie got top billing, Taylor's first feature impressed the MGM brass enough to win her a contract. Her parents, however, firmly rejected several studio recommendations, including: changing Elizabeth's name to Virginia, dying her hair chestnut or red, and having her famous mole removed. Eventually, the studio backed off and Taylor became a full-fledged star in 1944's *National Velvet.*

Unlike her *National Velvet* co-star Mickey Rooney, Taylor didn't endure an awkward adolescence onscreen. If anything, she grew more beautiful, and at fourteen she was playing much older characters. Her adult career truly kicked into high gear in 1951, when George Stevens cast Taylor opposite Montgomery Clift in *A Place in the Sun.* As the rich heiress Angela, she gave a delicate, emotionally nuanced performance that forever lifted her status from ingénue to bona fide leading lady.

Taylor as Melinda Greyton in Conspirator (1949) — her first role as a leading lady.

FILM NOIR TOUGH GUYS

Inspired by the German Expressionist filmmakers of the twenties, directors of the 1940s cloaked their crime dramas in ominous chiaroscuro effects of shadow and light. Known as "film noir," these films depict the underbelly of American society — a world where corruption is rampant, ethics are subjective, and the line between heroes and villains is blurred. The following actors became stars in the atmospheric, hard-boiled film noir thrillers of the forties.

Alan Ladd was an exceptional high school athlete who got his start hanging around studio lots looking for work. He signed on as a grip before landing his first on-screen part as an extra in *Once in a Lifetime* in 1932. He won a larger role in the 1933 film, *Saturday's Millions,* and his film career was launched. Although short in stature, Ladd brought a snarling intensity and menace to a series of memorable tough guy roles. His breakthrough role came in the 1942 crime drama, *This Gun for Hire,* where he plays a hardened contract killer on the run with Veronica Lake.

Burt Lancaster, the son of a New York City postal worker, was a spectacular high school athlete before he decided to hit the road as half of a successful acrobatic team. World War II intervened, however, and when he returned home, he found himself on Broadway. After a brief stage stint, Lancaster made his screen debut in the 1946 film, *The Killers,* a loose adaptation of Ernest Hemingway's short story. He followed this star-making performance with such noir classics as *Brute Force* (1947) and *Criss Cross* (1949).

Robert Mitchum was a fatherless child who found adventure in a variety of jobs before he discovered acting. While working at Lockheed Aircraft he joined the Long Beach Theater Guild and soon gravitated to Hollywood. Mitchum's first film was *Hoppy Serves a Writ* in 1943, and he kept active in a series of Hopalong Cassidy westerns, appearing in eighteen movies in 1943 alone. His breakthrough role came in 1945 in *The Story of G.I. Joe,* which earned him an Academy Award nomination for Best Supporting Actor. Two years later, Mitchum became a star in the classic noir thriller, *Out of the Past.*

(top to bottom)
Alan Ladd,
Burt Lancaster
(with Ava Gardner),
Robert Mitchum

OTHER STARS OF THE PERIOD

Lauren Bacall   Montgomery Clift

Lauren Bacall, whose father was a traveling salesman and mother a secretary, was born Betty Joan Perske in the Bronx on September 16, 1924. After attending the American Academy of Dramatic Arts, Bacall split her time between minor Broadway roles and modeling. Fate intervened when director Howard Hawks's wife noticed the stunning beauty on the cover of *Harper's Bazaar*. She tipped off her husband and before long, Bacall was starring opposite Humphrey Bogart in the 1944 film, *To Have and Have Not*. It was an auspicious debut that led to her being dubbed "The Look," because of her irresistible, seductive gaze.

Montgomery Clift began his career on the stage in summer stock and Broadway. Hollywood came calling early, but he remained in New York until 1948, when he made his screen debut as a compassionate American GI helping a young Czech war orphan in Fred Zinnemann's *The Search* (1948). Nominated for a Best Actor Oscar for *The Search*, Clift surprised many by then starring opposite John Wayne in Howard Hawks's *Red River* (1948). An intense, driven actor who preferred the stage to cinema, Clift nonetheless starred in such classics as *A Place in the Sun* (1951) and *From Here to Eternity* (1953).

Ava Gardner grew up dirt poor in rural North Carolina. A photograph of the beautiful brunette taken on a trip to New York eventually brought the farmer's daughter to MGM for a screen test. In 1941 Gardner appeared in her first film, *H.M. Pulham, Esq*. A few years later, after her seductive role in *The Killers*, she would become Hollywood's leading sex symbol — "The World's Most Beautiful Animal."

Alec Guinness   Frank Sinatra   Orson Welles   Shelley Winters

Alec Guinness, recognized the world over as a supremely talented stage and screen actor, was born Alec Guinness de Cuffe on April 2, 1914, in London. He got his start on the British stage before heading to America, where he continued his stage success. His first substantial movie appearance was in the 1946 David Lean film, *Great Expectations,* but Guinness's true film debut came twelve years earlier as an extra in 1934's *Evensong.* He became a star after playing Fagin in Lean's *Oliver Twist* (1948) and astonished filmgoers by playing no less than eight different characters in the black comedy, *Kind Hearts and Coronets* (1949).

Jennifer Jones, born Phyllis Isley on March 2, 1919, toured the country with her vaudevillian parents and later acted in stock theater productions. After attending the American Academy of Dramatic Arts in New York, Jones moved to Hollywood where she easily found work playing leads in minor westerns and action films. Her first film in 1939 was *New Frontier,* followed closely by *Dick Tracy's G-Men* the same year. When producer David O. Selznick saw her performance, he gave her the lead in 1943's *The Song of Bernadette,* her first film under the name Jennifer Jones. She received an Academy Award for Best Actress and went on to marry Selznick in 1949.

Frank Sinatra was a skinny teen idol from Hoboken, New Jersey, with a knack for driving bobby-soxers wild. Born on December 12, 1915, Sinatra dropped out of high school at fifteen to pursue his singing career. He eventually landed with the Tommy Dorsey Orchestra in 1940, and appeared with the band in two movies, *Las Vegas Nights* (1941) and *Ship Ahoy* (1942). After landing a contract at MGM, he finally debuted in his first major role in the musical, *Anchors Aweigh* (1945), which paired him with Gene Kelly. A natural actor with surprising range, Sinatra more than held his own against the charismatic Kelly and proved to be a decent hoofer. He would later win an Academy Award for Best Supporting Actor as the ill-fated Maggio in *From Here to Eternity* (1953).

Lana Turner, known as "The Sweater Girl", began her life in Wallace, Idaho, as Julia Jean Mildred Frances Turner. When her father died in a murder-robbery, she moved with her mother to California at the age of nine. Legend has it that Turner was discovered in Schwab's Drugstore wearing, of course, a snug-fitting sweater. Signed by MGM, she changed her first name to Lana and landed a bit part in the 1937 film, *A Star is Born.* She is best remembered for later roles in *The Postman Always Rings Twice* in 1946, and *Peyton Place,* which won her an Oscar nomination in 1957.

Orson Welles was a child prodigy who traveled to Ireland after high school to begin his acting career. By 1934, Welles had returned to the U.S. and landed on Broadway. That same year, he directed and starred in his first film, the four-minute short *Hearts of Age.* The rest of his career, of course, is legendary, as Welles was the man responsible for *The War of the Worlds* radio broadcast and *Citizen Kane* (1941), which was his feature film debut as director, writer, and star.

Shelley Winters, née Schrift, started acting in high school. By the age of nineteen, she had already made her Broadway debut. She acted in a series of plays before getting called out to Hollywood in 1943, where she made her big-screen debut in *What a Woman!* Her first substantial role came in 1947's *A Double Life,* where she plays the ill-fated mistress of an aging actor (Ronald Colman) teetering on the brink of a nervous breakdown. Usually cast as a sexpot in her early films, Winters reinvented herself as a blowzy character actress in *A Place in the Sun* (1951), which brought her an Oscar nomination. She successfully alternated between stage and screen, eventually winning Oscars for her roles in *The Diary of Anne Frank* (1959) and *A Patch of Blue* (1965).

(facing page) Lana Turner

1950-1969

CinemaScope widened the big screen for the first time in *The Robe* (1953), starring Richard Burton and Jean Simmons.

Classic Hitchcock film, *Dial M for Murder* (1954), starring Robert Cummings, Grace Kelly, and Ray Milland.

Cinerama, a grand cinematic experiment on display in the travelogue, Cinerama Holiday (1955).

THE THREAT OF TELEVISION AND THE DECLINE OF THE STUDIOS

The fifties ushered in a decade of unprecedented prosperity, but the outlook for the "dream factories" wasn't quite so promising. McCarthyism still gripped the film industry and the major studios were declining in power. Many of the legendary studio heads, like Louis B. Mayer and Harry Cohn, would be dead within the decade. More importantly, the rise of television threw the studios, filmmakers, and motion picture exhibitors into a panic.

Television's growing popularity dealt a heavy blow to the motion picture industry. Movie houses were virtually empty on Tuesday nights, thanks to the antics of former vaudeville comedian Milton Berle. On his *Texaco Star Theatre*, "Uncle Miltie" literally captured the entire nation's attention for one hour every week. Viewers also tuned in to the situation comedy *I Love Lucy* in record numbers. As Lucy and Ricky Ricardo, real-life couple Lucille Ball and Desi Arnaz became household names.

The motion picture industry responded to the threat of television with three technological weapons: Cinerama, 3-D, and CinemaScope. Cinerama debuted in 1952 with *This is Cinerama,* a travel documentary, which was shot with three cameras and shown with three interlocking projectors that cast their images on a curved, wraparound screen. By the mid-1960s the novelty had worn off and Cinerama was rare. The debut of 3-D came the same year as Cinerama with the low-budget movie, *Bwana Devil* (1952). While far less expensive than Cinerama, 3-D required audiences to wear uncomfortable red and green-tinted glasses to get the effect. By the end of the decade it, too, had disappeared.

CinemaScope, however, turned out to be a less-expensive widescreen technique than Cinerama. The first feature shot in CinemaScope was the biblical epic, *The Robe,* which 20th Century Fox released in major cities as a reserved-seat special event in 1953. A huge hit, The Robe ushered in a wave of big-screen, star-driven biblical spectacles, including Cecil B. DeMille's remake of *The Ten Commandments* (1956) and the Oscar winning *Ben-Hur* (1959).

The fifties also marked the beginning of the end for the Production Code. For nearly twenty years, rigid Code standards had forced filmmakers to excise anything deemed objectionable from their films. According to the Production Code, married couples slept in separate beds and crime did not pay. It was unheard-of to release a film without the Code's seal of approval. As a result, director Elia Kazan had to tone down the sexually charged material in his adaptation of Tennessee Williams's *A Streetcar Named Desire* (1951). This all changed, however, when maverick director Otto Preminger released the romantic comedy, *The Moon is Blue* (1953), without the Code's seal of approval. Hollywood braced for a backlash, but the film was a sizable hit. From then on, filmmakers began pushing the creative envelope, tackling taboo subjects such as drug addiction in *The Man With the Golden Arm* (1955), and sexuality in *Baby Doll* (1956).

Perhaps no star reflects the change in the Hollywood of the fifties more than Marlon Brando. One of the new breed of Method-trained actors, Brando set the stage for James Dean and Paul Newman, who made their debuts in *East of Eden* (1955) and *The Silver Chalice* (1954) respectively. Dean, in particular, became a symbol for the decade's misunderstood youth, who flocked to his film, *Rebel Without a Cause* (1956) when it was released following Dean's death in a car accident.

The lushly beautiful and sensitive Marilyn Monroe shot to stardom in *Gentlemen Prefer Blondes* (1953) and Billy Wilder's *The Seven Year Itch* (1955). Gene Kelly in *An American in Paris* (1951) and *Singin' in the Rain* (1952) re-established the musical in the fifties. By decade's end, Hollywood seemed to have regained some of its luster.

The cultural and social status quo of the fifties was completely upended in the sixties when the counterculture forever shattered the established order. Hollywood also endured both financial and artistic upheaval. The studio system gave way to the rise of the studio-financed, independently produced domestic films. Corporate mergers swallowed up many of the studios, which became part of vast entertainment conglomerates.

Despite the social changes sweeping the country, Hollywood, for the most part, tried to play it safe churning out wholesome, crowd-pleasing films that bore little resemblance to reality. As one overblown and over-budget musical after another bombed at the box office, the cost-conscious studios began cutting back on production across the board. A critical and commercial flop, the $40 million epic, *Cleopatra* (1963) nearly sank 20th Century Fox. Many of the decade's expensive costume dramas, like *Doctor Zhivago* (1965) and *The Lion in Winter* (1968), were produced overseas. Studio film production ultimately hit an all-time low in the late sixties.

There were still profits to be made, however. The longest-running franchise in film history began with the 1962 release of *Doctor No,* which introduced the character of British secret agent James Bond. Its star, Sean Connery, became an international superstar bringing Agent 007 to the screen in the first five films in the series.

MGM released Stanley Kubrick's ambitious science fiction epic, *2001: A Space Odyssey* in 1968 to initially confused audiences. Whereas Kubrick turned his attention to the future, many sixties-era filmmakers focused resolutely on the present. Mike Nichols' sleeper hit, *The Graduate* (1967) wittily captures the confusion and disenchantment of a recent college graduate in upper middle-class California. Dennis Hopper's *Easy Rider* (1969) depicts the hatred and fear that the counterculture engendered in middle America. And famed cinematographer Haskell Wexler blurs the line between reality and fantasy with his directorial debut in *Medium Cool* (1968), which uses actual footage of the anarchy surrounding the 1968 Democratic National Convention in Chicago.

In 1969, the Academy Awards gave the coveted Best Picture award to *Midnight Cowboy,* an X-rated film whose main characters are a two-bit street hustler and a naïve male prostitute. It appeared that even the Hollywood establishment could no longer ignore the social and political changes of the decade.

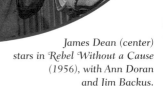

James Dean (center) stars in *Rebel Without a Cause* (1956), with Ann Doran and Jim Backus.

Elizabeth Taylor earned the movies' first million-dollar salary in *Cleopatra* (1963).

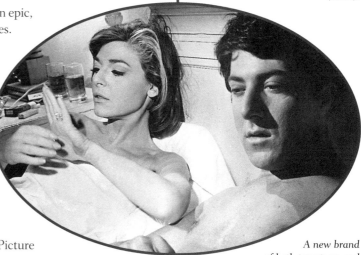

A new brand of both temptress and movie hero emerged in Mike Nichols' *The Graduate* (1967), with Anne Bancroft and Dustin Hoffman (his first leading role).

WOODY ALLEN

From his first role in *What's New, Pussycat?* (1965), the angst-ridden Woody Allen has become one of the most recognizable figures in contemporary screen comedy. Over the years, Allen has famously mined his Brooklyn childhood, Jewish heritage, and urban neuroses for comic material. Resolutely anti-Hollywood, he is a prolific filmmaker who writes, directs, and stars in films that resist easy categorization. His comic sensibility tends to swing between two poles: broad, silly slapstick and cerebral, literate farce that both celebrates and affectionately skewers the intelligentsia.

Contrary to what fans have surmised from his Oscar-winning masterpiece *Annie Hall*, Allen did not grow up living next to a Coney Island roller coaster. Born Allen Stewart Konigsberg on December 1, 1935, in Brooklyn, Allen began writing gags for New York columnists Walter Winchell and Herb Lyons while still in high school. He soon branched out from gag writing and began honing his unique brand of stand-up comedy in the small clubs of Greenwich Village, where Allen brought a distinctly intellectual edge to his work. Recordings and subsequent appearances on *The Tonight Show* brought him further renown and a national audience.

Allen's nightclub act caught the eye of film producer Charles K. Feldman, who was struggling to adapt the Czech farce *Lot's Wife* for the screen. Numerous writers had already attempted the difficult task of turning a very European farce into a broadly commercial movie, but none of the drafts had satisfied Feldman, who hoped Allen had the right comic sensibility for the job. Allen agreed to try to adapt the script. As extra incentive, Feldman told Allen that he could write a minor part for himself.

Allen as Victor Skakapopulis in his debut film, What's New Pussycat? *(1965).*

It was a painful and humbling introduction to the Hollywood filmmaking process for Allen, who wrote several versions of the script, only to see many of his jokes cut or reinterpreted by the film's director, Clive Donner. A classic mid-sixties film comedy, the newly named *What's New, Pussycat?* (1965) is an all-star, racy sex comedy packed with gags both juvenile and sophisticated. Wearing a Buster Brown wig, Peter Sellers plays an addled psychiatrist who is treating the chronic womanizer, Peter O'Toole.

Despite his long-standing engagement, O'Toole's character can't resist a few last dalliances before resigning himself to marriage. Allen enters the comic fray as Victor Skakapopulis, a neurotic loser who envies O'Toole's success with women.

Despite the film's commercial success, Allen was somewhat disappointed with the final version of *What's New, Pussycat?* Many of his favorite lines had been left out from the script he supplied. From this point on, he insisted on creative control over all future scripts. It was certainly an ambitious pledge by a novice filmmaker with only one credit on his resume. Nevertheless, by keeping his costs low and staying far away from studio interference, Allen has been able to honor that pledge since he began directing and writing his own movies, starting the very next year with *What's Up, Tiger Lily?*

Allen with Pussycat *co-stars Romy Schneider and Peter O'Toole.*

(facing page) Allen in a 1963 publicity shot for a guest appearance on the hit TV show Candid Camera.

MARLON BRANDO

Brando as a young boy.

Brando as a wheelchair-bound ex-GI in The Men (1950), his film debut.

Marlon Brando made a name for himself in Hollywood in the fifties playing marginal, rebellious anti-heroes. From Stanley Kowalski in *A Streetcar Named Desire* to Johnny Strabler in *The Wild One* and through five decades of acting excellence, Brando has demonstrated an unparalleled ability to access the primitive, emotional core of his characters. One of Hollywood's most acclaimed performers, he has also been one of its most piercing critics, once quoted as saying, "The only reason I'm in Hollywood is that I don't have the moral courage to refuse the money." In 1972, his riveting, iconic performance as Don Vito Corleone in *The Godfather* was recognized with an Academy Award for Best Actor, but Brando, the perennial outsider, refused to accept the Oscar and in fact did not even show up for the ceremony. His notorious disdain for Hollywood politics combined with his profound dedication to his craft has contributed to Brando's mystique as modern cinema's most magnetic – and enigmatic – performer.

He was born on April 2, 1924, in Omaha, Nebraska. Expelled from several schools as an unruly, often violent youngster, he found his direction when his mother, a devoted follower of the theater, suggested acting as an outlet for his pent-up emotion and aggression. His experience in local theater productions proved cathartic. With his mother's encouragement and his father's financial backing, he left Omaha to study acting in New York City.

Brando arrived in New York just as a new style of acting was gaining a foothold in theater. Inspired by the teachings of Russian actor Konstantin Stanislavsky, acting coaches Stella Adler and Lee Strasberg were leading workshops in the "Method," which emphasized emotional authenticity over the old school artificial techniques. Though he had little legitimate acting experience, Brando had an uncanny ability to tap into his emotions. He enrolled in an acting workshop at the New School for Social Research and quickly established himself as a dynamic, idiosyncratic actor.

His rise to stage success was rapid and relentless. After several acclaimed performances on Broadway, including a part in the wholesome family drama *I Remember Mama*, Brando landed the breakthrough role of Stanley Kowalski in a production of Tennessee Williams's *A Streetcar Named Desire*. According to Williams's memoirs, Brando gave the single greatest reading the playwright had ever heard; the young actor instantly captured the character's brutal sexuality and menacing physicality without turning him into a caricature. Playing opposite Jessica Tandy's emotionally fragile Blanche DuBois, Brando gave a performance that thrilled both critics and Broadway audiences, who had never seen anything quite like him onstage. The toast of Broadway, he was soon deluged with Hollywood offers. He initially snubbed all of them, including that of acclaimed producer Stanley Kramer.

Kramer refused to concede defeat. He barraged Brando with daily phone calls, even while the actor was vacationing in Paris. He followed up his phone calls by sending Brando a script for *The Men* (1950), which depicts a paralyzed and emotionally scarred World War II veteran's strained relationship with his long-suffering fiancée. Kramer, known for his liberal politics and commitment to social issues, believed that the role would appeal to the actor's anti-establishment sensibility and preference for challenging, provocative material.

Kramer's hunch proved correct. Brando agreed to make his film debut as the paralyzed veteran opposite Teresa Wright. It certainly helped that *The Men* was an independent film and not some glitzy studio production. To prepare for the physical and emotional demands of the role, Brando checked into a veterans' hospital for a month, getting firsthand experience of

WARNER BROS. STUDIOS
WARDROBE TEST
FOR
'A STREETCAR NAMED DESIRE' 372

OF
M BRANDO
AS
STANLEY

WARDROBE CHANGE # 9
SET { INT STELLA'S FLAT
WORN IN { SCENE 116

8·9·50

the isolation and pain of paralysis. By the time production began, he was equipped to bring an incredible degree of authenticity to his part. Under Fred Zinnemann's sensitive direction, Brando delivers a performance that critics hailed as gritty, honest, and true.

A string of marquee roles soon followed, including a film reprise of his role in *Streetcar* and the leads in *Viva Zapata!* (1952) and *On the Waterfront* (1954). Brando earned three Oscar nominations in his first five film outings and eventually won the Best Actor award for *On the Waterfront*.

> "The only reason I'm in Hollywood is that I don't have the moral courage to refuse the money."
> — Marlon Brando

SEAN CONNERY

The actor who became famous for his portrayals of Ian Fleming's worldly, sophisticated secret agent James Bond was actually born into a lower-class neighborhood of Edinburgh, Scotland, on August 25, 1930. Thomas Sean Connery began working at the age of nine and quit school at thirteen to work full-time as a day laborer. At the age of fifteen, he enlisted for a twelve-year tour of duty in the British navy, only to be discharged after three years when he developed severe stomach ulcers. Faced with the bleak prospects of further manual labor jobs back home in Edinburgh, where he briefly laid bricks and polished coffins to make ends meet, Connery focused on bodybuilding and his dedication eventually earned him a trip to the 1950 Mr. Universe competition in London, where he placed third.

At the time of the competition, Connery still clung to his boyhood dream of playing professional soccer. He had never even considered the thought of acting as a career, but while in London, he auditioned on a whim for a traveling production of the musical *South Pacific*. Much to his surprise, he was offered a part in the chorus as a singing sailor. Feeling that the name Tommy was inappropriate for the professional stage, Connery opted to drop his first name altogether. He has been known as Sean Connery ever since.

His rise to fame was hardly meteoric. He followed his role in *South Pacific* with steady work as a stage actor, all the while taking classes to improve his acting skills. He made his first film appearance as an extra in the 1955 romantic fantasy *Let's Make Up,* which stars Anna Neagle and Errol Flynn. Connery's first speaking role in a feature film came in the 1957 British B-movie crime drama *No Road Back,* which stars American actor Skip Homeier. Based on the play *Madam Tic-Tac, No Road Back* features Connery as Spike, the muscular henchman for the film's villain (Alfie Bass). It was a small role that required Connery to do little more than glower and spit out a few lines of dialogue. Released by RKO to critical and public indifference in 1957, *No Road Back* was neither a setback nor a boon for Connery, who found more rewarding work in television. His performance as an aging boxer in a live broadcast of Rod Serling's *Requiem for a Heavyweight* earned him a number of offers, including a proposed five-year contract with 20th Century Fox.

Although he began collecting a salary immediately, the deal brought Connery no immediate work. Eventually, 20th Century Fox assigned Connery a small role in the MGM-produced *Action of the Tiger* (1957), a story of political intrigue starring Martine Carol and Van Johnson and directed by Terence Young. His part, that of a drunken, abusive sailor, was small and the movie unmemorable, but it was his first movie shot in color and he was certain that *Action of the Tiger* would jump-start his budding film career.

Connery's youthful enthusiasm impressed Terence Young, as did the appreciation of his co-star Martine Carol, who remarked that Connery should have taken Van Johnson's place as the movie's tough guy lead. But Young knew that *Action of the Tiger,* which was a disaster of a movie, would never get Connery the attention he deserved. To curb Connery's disappointment, Young vowed that he would try to help him. Five years later he directed him in *Dr. No,* the first installment of the James Bond franchise that would make Connery a global superstar.

Connery's first speaking part in No Road Back (1957), a British B-movie crime drama.

Connery with Ursula Andress in his first turn as James Bond in Dr. No (1962).

JAMES DEAN

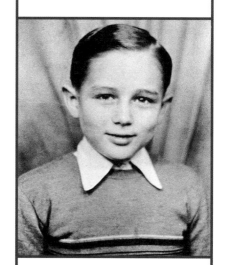

Dean as a young boy.

*Dean in one of
his first bit roles in
Has Anybody Seen My Gal? (1952).*

A sense of foreboding hangs over James Dean's movies, even when viewed today. The embodiment of fifties-era angst and rebellion, Dean brought to the screen an emotional urgency and hunger for connection that surpassed anything previously achieved by the famed members of the Method acting school. His death in a fiery car crash in 1955 gave birth to a cult following that time and nostalgia have elevated to the status of pop culture myth. Both the angry young man and the doomed romantic hero, Dean continues to exert an enduring fascination for moviegoers. A devout admirer of Marlon Brando and Montgomery Clift, Dean expanded the naturalistic approach to screen acting to the emotional extreme. The body of work he left behind is small, but the impact of it is undeniable. In only a handful of starring roles, he created scenes of unsurpassed emotional rawness, such as the nakedly vulnerable plea for his father's affection in *East of Eden* (1955). To this day, few scenes in all of cinema are more disturbing to watch.

The anguish that Dean so vividly expresses onscreen has its roots in the actor's painful childhood in the Depression-era Midwest. Born on February 8, 1931, in Marion, Indiana, Dean was extremely close to his mother, with whom he sang songs, danced, and told stories. When she died of ovarian cancer when he was nine, his cold, distant father left the boy to be raised by his aunt and uncle. Devastated and confused, Dean immersed himself in sports, farming, and motorcycling. But by the end of high school, acting proved to be his greatest ambition, and he headed to Southern California to pursue an acting career.

At Santa Monica City College, Dean practiced his diction by reciting Shakespeare soliloquies from *Hamlet*, a character with whom the brooding and rebellious teen had little trouble identifying. Then in 1950, he saw Marlon Brando's debut film, *The Men*. Brando's naturalistic, raw performance deeply affected the aspiring actor, who subsequently enrolled in a Method acting class in Los Angeles.

That December, nineteen-year-old Dean made his first filmed appearance in a Pepsi commercial. Several small film, television, and radio roles followed, including work as an extra in the Martin and Lewis comedy *Sailor Beware* (1951). His first film role came the following autumn in famed director Samuel Fuller's war drama called *Fixed Bayonets,* but his one line was eventually edited out. In 1952, Dean's film career officially began with a small part as a soda fountain customer in the otherwise unmemorable musical comedy *Has Anyone Seen My Gal?*

Unable to land more film work, Dean moved to New York and eventually landed a minor but crucial role as an Arab gigolo in a Broadway production of André Gide's *The Immoralist*. His performance impressed screenwriter Paul Osborn, who was then adapting John Steinbeck's sprawling family saga *East of Eden* for director Elia Kazan. Osborn convinced Kazan to let Dean audition for the part of Cal Trask, the wayward son of a stern Salinas Valley lettuce farmer. But Kazan had long envisioned Brando in the role, and rising Broadway star Paul Newman was also in the running. Dean's reading of the part was so impressive that Kazan hired him over the two more bankable stars, and Warner Brothers soon signed the

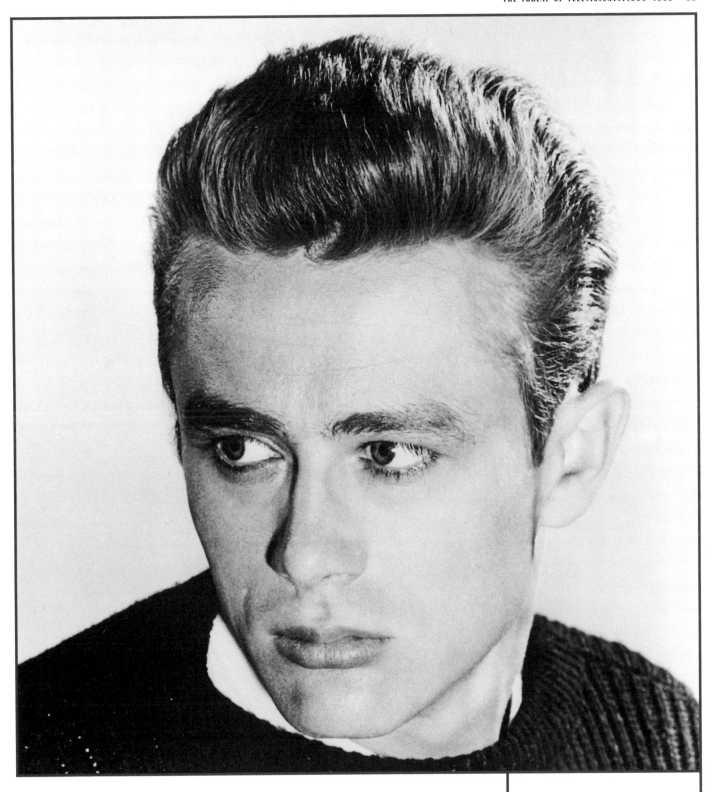

relative unknown to star opposite Julie Harris and veteran character actor Raymond Massey in *East of Eden*. Dean's searing performance in the critically acclaimed drama brought the 23-year-old actor both instant fame and an Academy Award nomination for Best Actor.

His next role, as confused teenager Jim Stark in Nicholas Ray's *Rebel Without a Cause* (1955), would further establish a youth following that lasts to this day. Tragically, he would be dead a little over a year after the premiere. While driving his Porsche Spider to Salinas, California, he lost control and was killed in the ensuing crash. His performance in *Giant,* on which he had finished working before his death, would be recognized with a posthumous Oscar nomination.

> **"He had the greatest power of concentration I have ever encountered."**
>
> — Jim Backus,
> Dean's *Rebel Without a Cause* castmate

CLINT EASTWOOD

With his rough-hewn features and stoic bearing, Eastwood gives little away onscreen. Emotionally terse, he radiates an integrity and grim resolve that give his characters instant credibility. Over the course of his nearly fifty-year career, the quiet man, whose first breaks came in spaghetti westerns, has refined his stoic loner persona into an internationally recognized archetype.

A child of the Depression, Clinton Eastwood Jr. was born in San Francisco on May 31, 1930. With money scarce and job prospects slim, his family traveled around northern California for most of Eastwood's childhood, stopping only where there were jobs. Eastwood's rootless existence finally came to an end when the family settled in Oakland, California.

Socially awkward and somewhat gawky in his 6-foot-4-inch frame, Eastwood went to Oakland Technical High School. An introverted outsider, he panicked and nearly skipped school to avoid going onstage when forced by his English teacher to play the lead in a school play. Once he overcame his stage fright, however, Eastwood surprised himself by actually enjoying the experience.

After working a series of menial jobs around the northwest, Eastwood joined the army and was stationed in southern California. Had he gone to Korea like most of his fellow trainees, he might never have given acting another thought. But with a newfound confidence, Eastwood charmed his way into a job as the Fort Ord swimming instructor. At the urging of two of his friends from the base, he attended an open audition at Universal Studios. After waiting two agonizing weeks, he received a call from Universal offering him a trial six-month contract.

Eastwood in his first credited role as Jonesy in Francis in the Navy (1955).

Eastwood spent all of his first six months with Universal in an actors' training program, learning to ride like a cowboy, dine like a gentleman, and duel like a pirate. Impressed by his affability and his eagerness to learn about movies, Universal executives renewed his contract and awarded him his first role as a bumbling lab technician named Jennings in *Revenge of the Creature* (1955), the sequel to *The Creature from the Black Lagoon* (1954). Production began on a sour note for Eastwood, who watched the film's director and producer quarrel over whether or not to cut his one scene. Even though the director grudgingly agreed to keep the scene, the young actor was all too aware that he was considered expendable. The scene is more memorable now because of Eastwood's Elvis-style pompadour than for his performance. As Jennings, Eastwood rattles off his lines while searching for a missing lab rat, which turns out to be hiding in his jacket pocket. While hardly an opportunity to showcase Eastwood's talents, *Revenge of the Creature* is now remembered, if at all, as the film that launched one of the great careers of modern cinema.

Eastwood in Francis in the Navy (1955), rescues Donald O'Connor.

Eastwood suffered through a couple of similarly small roles before landing the slightly more prominent role of Jonesy in *Francis in the Navy* (1955). He was listed in the credits for the first time and a few critics even paid him notice. Despite this modest success, Universal terminated his contract shortly after the film was released. Persevering through

a few more years of small, uncredited roles, Eastwood got his first really big break — the part of Rowdy Yates in the 1959 television western series *Rawhide*.

It was in this role that he began to fashion the strong, taciturn persona that he would make famous in Sergio Leone's spaghetti westerns starting with *A Fistful of Dollars* (1964). Eastwood later invested the same moodiness to the role of Harry Callahan in the *Dirty Harry* series, which made him one of the world's biggest box office draws. Though Eastwood has been ignored by critics for many years, his talents have finally been recognized by the establishment. In 1992 Eastwood won the Academy Award for Best Director for his western *Unforgiven*, which also took the Best Picture Award.

> **"My old drama coach used to say, 'Don't just do something, stand there.' Gary Cooper wasn't afraid to do nothing."**
>
> — Clint Eastwood

AUDREY HEPBURN

> **"I liked her a lot, in fact, I loved Audrey. It was easy to love her."**
>
> — Gregory Peck,
> Hepburn's *Roman Holiday* co-star

With her lithe figure, delicate features and natural grace, Audrey Hepburn stands in stark contrast to the buxom voluptuousness of such fifties-era stars as Marilyn Monroe and Sophia Loren. The epitome of chic, she nonetheless projects a warmth and naturalness that enables her to play a wide range of roles. Perhaps best known today for playing restless party girl Holly Golightly in *Breakfast at Tiffany's* (1961), Hepburn was a favorite with both audiences and directors such as Billy Wilder and William Wyler.

Edda Kathleen van Heemstra Hepburn-Ruston was born in Brussels, Belgium, on May 4, 1929. The only daughter of a successful British financier and a Dutch baroness, Hepburn's upbringing was every bit as pampered as her regal-sounding name suggests. When her parents divorced when she was ten, her mother brought her to London to attend an expensive boarding school for girls. There she learned the social graces and impeccable etiquette that would later become an integral part of her screen persona.

Hepburn's social privileges, however, failed to insulate her from the ravages of World War II. She was on vacation from school with her mother in Arnem, Holland, when the German army captured the resort town. As a consequence, she endured food shortages and a pervasive sense of hopelessness. It was not until the war's end that Hepburn and her mother returned to England.

Hepburn focused her energy on dance when she returned to London. Soon after, she won a scholarship to a dancing academy, where she impressed several modeling agents. On one modeling assignment she caught the eye of Dutch movie producer Charles van der Linden, who cast her as an extra in the travel documentary *Nederlands in 7 Lessen*. She later had a few walk-on roles in British films, most notably in *The Lavender Hill Mob* (1951), but it was a chance meeting with a legendary French novelist that ultimately brought Hepburn to Hollywood's attention.

Hepburn met the eccentric French author Colette while vacationing on the French Riviera with her mother, A Broadway production of Colette's novel *Gigi* was in the works and Colette immediately insisted that Hepburn be cast in the lead role. Despite her inexperience, Hepburn was a hit with both critics and theater audiences.

Around the same time, Paramount director William Wyler was searching for an unknown to play a reluctant princess opposite Gregory Peck in the romantic comedy *Roman Holiday* (1953). When Wyler read the reviews of Hepburn's performance in *Gigi,* he requested a screen test. Although she came across as tense, Wyler secretly kept the cameras rolling after the formal test was over. Unaware that she was being filmed, Hepburn returned to her charming, unguarded self. According to Wyler, she was "absolutely delicious."

Paramount immediately signed her for *Roman Holiday.* Playing a sheltered princess who desperately wants to escape the confinements of her royal life, Hepburn called upon her dual experiences of privilege and privation during the War. Sneaking out of the palace, Hepburn's princess cuts her hair and finds a willing tour guide in American reporter Gregory Peck. Regally and exuberantly, Hepburn conveys her character's delight in the ordinary — the princess and reporter fall deeply in love. More than one reviewer called the results "magical." Hepburn's performance won her an Academy Award for Best Actress, beating out Deborah Kerr and Ava Gardner, among others.

That same year, Hepburn won a Tony Award for her performance as a water sprite in the Broadway production of *Ondine.* She went on to win four more Academy Award nominations for her roles in *Sabrina* (1954), *The Nun's Story* (1959), *Breakfast at Tiffany's* (1961), and *Wait Until Dark* (1967).

Hepburn, in one of her earliest films — *Young Wives' Tale* (1951).

Hepburn's stunning performance in the Broadway play *Gigi* (left) landed her a gig opposite Gregory Peck in her breakout film, *Roman Holiday* (1953) (below).

DUSTIN HOFFMAN

Before he landed the starring role in The Graduate (1967), Hoffman was cast in Madigan's Millions, which began filming in 1967, but wasn't released until 1969.

D ustin Hoffman's uncanny ability to reveal the depths of his characters and their circumstances has enabled him to defy conventional casting traditions. In roles ranging from naïve college graduate to harried divorced father to autistic savant, Hoffman has created a gallery of screen characters that has won him legions of fans and two Academy Awards.

A Los Angeles native, Hoffman was born on August 8, 1937, to a family that had been hit hard by the Depression. His father struggled to make a living as a furniture salesman while Hoffman's mother put aside her own acting ambitions to care for him and his brother. Despite the family's precarious finances, Hoffman enjoyed a relatively happy childhood. He often entertained his primary school peers with wild antics and began appearing in school plays in junior high school, where he debuted as Tiny Tim in *A Christmas Carol.*

At a college professor's suggestion, Hoffman began acting at the Pasadena Playhouse, where he befriended fellow actor Gene Hackman. The two eventually set out for New York in the hope of plying their skills on the Broadway stage. After seemingly endless auditions, Hoffman debuted on Broadway in a new production of *A Cook for Mr. General.* More offers were not forthcoming, however, and Hoffman rededicated himself to learning his craft. Several years of study with the famed acting coach Lee Strasberg paid off with roles in *Waiting for Godot* and *The Journey of the Fifth Horse,* for which Hoffman won a Best Actor Obie.

In 1967, while starring in the acclaimed Broadway farce *Eh?* Hoffman stepped before the movie camera for the first time in the films *The Tiger Makes Out* and *Madigan's Millions.* In *The Tiger Makes Out,* he portrays a hippie in director Arthur Hiller's adaption of playwright Murray Schisgal's hit Broadway comedy. Hoffman's role is small, but he formed an enduring friendship with Schisgal, who would later co-write Hoffman's hit film *Tootsie* (1982) and become his partner in their production company, Punch Productions.

Hoffman nabbed his first leading role in the spy comedy *Madigan's Millions,* which was shot on location in Rome. He plays a bumbling Internal Revenue Service agent who's on the trail of a mobster played by Cesar Romero. An often hilarious spoof of Hitchcock thrillers, the producers of *Madigan's Millions* held back releasing it until 1969, when they were able to cash in on Hoffman's fame in the wake of *The Graduate* and *Midnight Cowboy* (1969).

By the time Hoffman returned home from shooting *Madigan's Millions* in Italy, the buzz from his stage performance in *Eh?* had traveled all the way to Hollywood, where director Mike Nichols was preparing to cast *The Graduate.* Nichols invited Hoffman to audition for the part of Benjamin Braddock, a disaffected college athlete who has affairs with one of his parents' friends and her daughter.

Hoffman's audition was nearly a disaster. Studio producers had been pushing established star Robert Redford for the part, so Hoffman's chances looked slim. Furthermore, Braddock's character was written as a star athlete and Hoffman's slight build didn't seem to fit the part. These pressures, combined with the awkward love scene he was supposed to read, caused him to nervously flub several of his lines.

Hoffman, with Anne Bancroft, in the brilliant film The Graduate (1967).

Dustin Hoffman in Eh? *(1967), a Broadway play in which he was cast a few months before this film debut.*

Fortunately for Hoffman, Nichols had envisioned Braddock as a sensitive, troubled, easily flustered character. He wanted Braddock to come across as trying to do the right thing despite the lack of any clear moral signposts. As it turned out, Hoffman's nervousness convinced Nichols that he was perfect for the role. After winning the role, Hoffman grew more and more assured during production. His performance as Benjamin Braddock struck a chord with young audiences, who saw in Braddock's coming of age a reflection of their own experiences in the turbulent sixties. A sleeper at the box office, *The Graduate* brought Hoffman the first of his seven Oscar nominations.

ROCK HUDSON

When Hudson broke into Hollywood in the last days of the studio system in the late forties, the studio press corps carefully molded his image into a tall, dark, and handsome matinee idol, despite a well-known Hollywood secret — his homosexuality. Hudson went along with this elaborate masquerade until an AIDS diagnosis made it no longer tenable. An engaging, good-humored, light comedian, Hudson was also a credible dramatic actor whose compelling performances distinguished him from other matinee idols of the fifties. For his role in *Giant* (1956) as Jordan "Bick" Benedict, the former Roy Scherer Jr. from the affluent Chicago suburb of Winnetka, Illinois, received an Academy Award nomination.

Born on November 17, 1925, the son of an auto mechanic and a telephone operator, he was always interested in acting, but was held back by a chronic inability to remember lines. With the outbreak of World War II, Hudson left Winnetka to join the Navy as an airplane mechanic. After his discharge, he moved to Los Angeles, where he worked as a truck driver and poised himself to become an actor. His photograph found its way to the desk of veteran talent scout Henry Willson, who quickly signed the actor and began grooming him for stardom. Though Hudson was now using his stepfather's last name of Fitzgerald, Willson still didn't feel the name was star-worthy. After many suggestions, they finally settled on Rock Hudson.

At Willson's urging, he took acting and dancing classes and posed for dozens of publicity photos, some of which appeared in magazines even before he made his first film. Though eminently camera-ready, Hudson came across as inexperienced and awkward. After five screen tests, he was still not offered a studio contract. 20th Century Fox is rumored to still show his test today — as evidence that hard work can pay off for almost anyone.

Hudson finally got a break when Willson arranged a meeting for him with veteran director Raoul Walsh at Warner Brothers. Walsh agreed to give him a bit part in his 1948 film *Fighter Squadron.* In the film, Hudson plays an air corps officer stationed at an American base in England. Hudson has only three lines, one of which turned out to be a tongue-twister. It took 38 takes and a change in the wording before Hudson could say the line, "Pretty soon you're going to have to get a bigger blackboard." Walsh's patience ultimately paid off when producers saw the handsome newcomer on screen. Hudson was signed to a one-year contract, which was later picked up by Universal Pictures in 1949 for seven more years.

As a newcomer with little experience, Hudson was brought along slowly, working his way from bit parts to supporting roles. His first leading role came in 1952 opposite Yvonne De Carlo in *Scarlet Angel,* a low-budget western. Two years later, he was cast in Douglas Sirk's *Magnificent Obsession* as Robert Merrick, a drunken playboy who mends his ways after causing an accident which took the life of another doctor. He eventually becomes a respected surgeon, and falls in love with the physician's blind widow, played by Jane Wyman. A sentimental tearjerker, *Magnificent Obsession* firmly established Hudson as a romantic leading man and top box office attraction, a position he would occupy until the late sixties.

> **Hudson came across as inexperienced and awkward. He shot five screen tests, none of which brought the offer of a studio contract.**

Hudson at twenty, after returning home from World War II.

Hudson (far left), in his film debut in
Fighter Squadron (1948). Also
pictured (from left to right) are
Robert Stack, Edmund O'Brien, and
Walter Reed.

GRACE KELLY

> **"Hollywood amuses me. Holier-than-thou for the public and unholier-than-the-devil in reality."**
>
> — Grace Kelly

A young Kelly in an early publicity shot.

After a small role in Fourteen Hours (1951), Kelly (right) landed the part of Gary Cooper's wife in High Noon.

It seems only appropriate that Grace Kelly would eventually play blue-blood heiress Tracy Lord in *High Society* (1956), the musical version of *The Philadelphia Story* (1940). The third child of a wealthy construction contractor and a former high fashion model, Kelly needed to look no further than her own privileged upbringing for inspiration. Born November 29, 1929, in Philadelphia, Kelly was drawn to acting from an early age; she made her stage debut in a local play when she was only ten years old. Dramatic talent apparently ran in the family — her uncle was Pulitzer Prize-winning playwright George Kelly. When Grace was a teenager, her uncle arranged for her to attend New York's famous American Academy of Dramatic Arts.

Kelly's classically beautiful features prompted film offers with extraordinary rapidity, but she preferred to hone her technique in the theater. Having no intention of becoming a flash-in-the-pan movie starlet, she summarily rejected the allure of the movies, opting for a few roles in the fledgling medium of television to supplement her income. Finally, in 1949, Kelly landed a substantial role in a new Broadway production of August Strindberg's *The Father*. In one of her nightly performances, she caught the eye of film producer Sol Siegel, who promptly offered her a role in the thriller *Fourteen Hours* (1951). At her agent's prodding, Kelly reluctantly accepted Siegel's offer to make her film debut.

The plot of *Fourteen Hours* tracks the time a disturbed man spends contemplating suicide from a window ledge and focuses chiefly on a policeman's attempts to talk him down. The lives of ordinary people in the same building form a resonant emotional backdrop for the film's main action. Kelly portrays a woman consulting a divorce attorney. As she watches the unfolding suicide drama, she decides to give her marriage a second chance. Steering clear of sentiment, Kelly gives an emotionally restrained performance. Barely in her twenties at the time, she had a natural elegance and poise that enabled her to play much older characters. She came across as a woman, not a girlish ingénue.

While *Fourteen Hours* was not a commercial success, it did help Kelly land her breakthrough role in *High Noon* (1952). That film's screenwriter, Carl Foreman, watched *Fourteen Hours* and saw in her the refinement and emotional composure required of *High Noon's* female lead, a stoic Quaker bride to a frontier sheriff (Gary Cooper). Foreman convinced director Fred Zinnemann and producer Stanley Kramer to offer Kelly the plum role. Almost overnight, she became a nationally recognized star.

Two years later, Kelly starred in *Rear Window*, the first of three Alfred Hitchcock projects that would cement her status as a major talent. In 1954, she downplayed her looks to play Georgie, the frustrated wife of an alcoholic singer in *The Country Girl*. Kelly's performance won her an Academy Award and moved her to the top of Hollywood's A list. But her career ended almost as quickly as it began. She retired from acting in 1956 to marry Prince Rainier of Monaco. The stately bearing that had served Kelly so well on the screen was easily adapted to her new offscreen role as princess.

JACK LEMMON

In an era when stars reign for a decade or two before passing their crown to a young newcomer, Jack Lemmon is the exception. Since his Oscar-winning performance in *Mister Roberts* (1955) early on in his career, Lemmon has excelled in creating high-strung, energetic characters perfectly suited to mine the depths of comic exasperation from the scripts of Neil Simon and Billy Wilder, among others. His neurotic, put-upon heroes have often found their craggy foil in Walter Matthau, with whom he starred in eight movies, including *The Odd Couple* (1968) and *Grumpy Old Men* (1993).

As would befit one of his anxiety-plagued characters, Lemmon was born prematurely in a Newton, Massachusetts, hospital elevator on February 8, 1925. The only child of a bakery president and a socialite, Lemmon attended the prestigious Andover Academy, where he discovered both the piano and the stage. A good student, Lemmon went on to Harvard, but was dismayed to find that the university offered no theater courses. He therefore pursued his acting ambitions by joining two extracurricular clubs — the Harvard Dramatic Club and the Hasty Pudding Club.

Following college and naval service, Lemmon headed to Broadway and played piano in the Knickerbocker Music Hall to pay the rent. Unable to find stage work, he took a role on the radio drama *The Brighter Day*. From there he found work in television in the 1949 situation comedy *That Wonderful Guy*. Set in New York, the series depicts the comic misadventures of an aspiring actor who becomes the houseboy for a respected drama critic. The series ran only 17 weeks, but the show was not a total loss for Lemmon. Cincinnati Post critic Mary Wood wrote that the show "stars an obscure, but wonderful, comedian named Jack Lemmon." He had no problem finding regular television work and starred with his then-wife Cynthia Stone in another sitcom, *Heavens for Betsy*.

In March of 1954, Max Arnow, head of talent for Columbia Pictures, saw Lemmon in a stage revival of *Room Service*. Looking for someone to play the romantic lead in a Judy Holliday film, Arnow tested him for the part. The screen test was filmed by novice director Richard Quine, who later said, "I adored Lemmon from the first moment. He had that quality about him." Columbia executives were equally enthusiastic and Lemmon made his big screen debut in *It Should Happen to You* (1954).

In this romantic comedy written by Garson Kanin, Lemmon plays Pete, a filmmaker shooting a documentary in Central Park, where he meets model Gladys Clover (Judy Holliday). Out of work, she tries to get publicity by putting her name on billboards all over New York. Suddenly, she is in demand and Pete must compete with a wealthy playboy (Peter Lawford) for her attentions.

Both the movie and Lemmon were a hit with audiences. He appeared in just two more films before landing the plum role of Ensign Frank Pulver in *Mister Roberts* in 1955. Since winning the Best Supporting Actor Oscar for *Mister Roberts*, Jack Lemmon has been nominated seven more times and won Best Actor for 1973's *Save the Tiger*. His career continued to flourish well into his seventies, until his untimely death in 2001.

> **"I adored Lemmon from the first moment. He had that quality about him."**
>
> — Director Richard Quine

Lemmon was also a pretty good piano player. For a while, he made ends meet by playing in a New York City beer hall.

Lemmon's big screen debut — as Pete Sheppard (opposite Judy Holliday) in It Should Happen to You (1954).

JERRY LEWIS

"People hate me because
I am a multi-faceted,
talented, wealthy,
internationally
famous genius."

— Jerry Lewis,
joking about himself.

Before movie stardom, young Lewis made radio audiences laugh with his nightclub partner, Dean Martin.

Martin and Lewis — a duo that had performed their successful comedy routine on stage throughout the country — made their film debut in My Friend Irma (1949).

Whether working with straight man Dean Martin or on his own, comedian Jerry Lewis generates a raucous, anarchic comic energy. Known for his manic physical comedy and shameless mugging, Lewis is also an acclaimed writer and director whom straight-faced French critics regard as a comic genius. As Lewis himself once remarked in jest, "People hate me because I am a multifaceted, talented, wealthy, internationally famous genius."

A performer in his father's vaudeville theater starting at age five, Lewis was born Jerome Levitch on March 16, 1926, in Newark, New Jersey. While Lewis had substantial singing talents, it was clear from an early stage that comedy was his greatest strength. By the time he entered high school, he had developed an original comedy routine containing most of the key elements of the juvenile screen persona that would eventually make him a star.

After being expelled from high school for punching the principal, reportedly in response to an anti-Semitic remark, Lewis took his act to Atlantic City's nightclubs. There he met future partner Dean Martin, who was working as a lounge singer. The two men were matched immediately, with Martin's good looks and self-assured charm providing the necessary foil to Lewis's frenetic man-child act. They quickly became the star attraction on the Boardwalk and beyond. By the end of the 1940s, Martin and Lewis were the nation's favorite comedy team.

After seeing their act, Paramount producer Hal Wallis quickly moved to sign Martin and Lewis to a contract. At the time, however, Wallis lacked the right vehicle to introduce them as screen personalities. With the producer's encouragement, the pair was more than willing to wait for the right opportunity. A few months later, Paramount bought the screen rights to the popular television show *My Friend Irma*. Wallis arranged for the script to incorporate Lewis and Martin as comically feuding juice vendors.

When Wallis brought the comic team to Beverly Hills for their screen tests, Martin breezed through his straight man role without a hitch. Lewis, on the other hand, was asked to depart from his stage act to play an arrogant con artist. After a long day of retakes, both Lewis and director George Marshall were nearly ready to give up. He just couldn't seem to play the type. Luckily, at his wife's suggestion, the young comic proposed abandoning the scripted character in favor of his energetic, loud-mouthed, juvenile nightclub persona. Lewis refined the idea in collaboration with writer Cy Howard, renaming the character Seymour and giving him some new signature quirks. The results were a remarkable improvement. While the romance between Irma and Martin's character Steve Laird is the focus of the movie's plot, Martin and Lewis steal scenes with their comic rapport. They were such a hit with audiences that Wallis expanded their roles in the sequel *My Friend Irma Goes West* (1950).

Martin and Lewis made thirteen more films together before going their separate ways in the mid-fifties. Their split gave Lewis the opportunity to continue developing his peculiar brand of comedy, most notably in *The Nutty Professor* (1963), which is widely hailed as the actor/director/writer's finest film.

SOPHIA LOREN

The screen's quintessential bombshell is far more than a sex object. Unlike many of her sultry contemporaries whose careers have faded or whose roles have changed with their advancing years, Sophia Loren is still above all an actress, willing to appear as drab or as glamorous as the roles require. Nonetheless, her sex appeal has not faded, nor has her box office draw paled.

The daughter of an unwed mother, Loren was born into a life of poverty in Rome on September 20, 1934. Growing up in the ghettoes of Naples, she had to struggle against not only indigence, but also the stigma of being an illegitimate child in Catholic Italy. World War II made food and money even more scarce. With no place else to go, Loren and her mother were often forced to take shelter in railway tunnels while Allied bombers wreaked havoc.

Until she hit puberty, she was known around her neighborhood as "Sophia Toothpick" or simply "The Stick." But when the war ended and food rations were abandoned, Loren blossomed. In 1948, at fourteen years old, she began entering beauty pageants with the hope of becoming an actress and earning a living. After she won several Naples-area competitions, Loren's prospects seemed promising enough to warrant a move to Rome. It was there, in 1949, that she was discovered by movie producer Carlo Ponti, who served as a judge for a pageant in which she placed second. Ponti soon discovered Loren was possessed of a personal charisma equal to her physical appeal. He arranged for her to study with several noted acting coaches and eventually used his connections to set up a series of screen tests, but none immediately persuaded casting directors to give her a chance. As a result, Loren only found work as an extra in a series of small Italian productions and MGM's epic *Quo Vadis* (1951), which was filmed on location in Italy.

Ponti stuck by her, however, and in 1952 Loren landed her first substantial role in film. When the Phoenix production company issued a casting call for an actress to star in its upcoming B-movie *Africa Under the Seas,* Loren's mother saw the advertisement and notified Ponti, who arranged for Loren to meet with producer Goffredo Lombardo. Loren was apprehensive entering the meeting because she knew that the part required an actress who could swim, which she was unable to do. Nevertheless, at her mother's urging, she claimed to swim "like a champion" and won the role.

Filming began on a rather embarrassing note for Loren, who froze when the director ordered her to jump from the rail of an ocean liner into the sea. She refused, finally divulging her inability to swim. The director was furious, but it was too late to recast the role, so he insisted that Loren learn. Initially, she would jump from the boat and be retrieved by expert swimmers. However, in order to act in the film's many underwater scenes, she was forced to learn to become a fully proficient scuba diver.

Ponti continued to look for the right vehicle to launch Loren's career. Following *Africa Under the Seas,* she accepted the title role in the screen version of Verdi's opera *Aida* (1953). Dubbed by opera singer Renata Tebaldi, Loren plays the Ethiopian slave who falls in love with an Egyptian soldier during the reign of the pharaohs.

Shortly after these films, Loren gave her most impressive performance to date in Vittorio De Sica's comic anthology *The Gold of Naples* (1954). Her performance as an unfaithful wife looking for her wedding ring captured the attention of Hollywood, which resulted in her being cast in a series of four American films shot abroad, usually in the role of an exotic sexpot. She returned to Italy and gave a bravura performance as a rape victim in the 1961 drama *Two Women.* Hailed by critics, Loren made Academy Award history by becoming the first performer to win an Oscar for a foreign-language film.

Loren receiving her first Communion.

> **Until she hit puberty, she was known around her neighborhood as "Sophia Toothpick."**

Loren in one of her earliest leading roles — the title role of Aida (1953).

MARILYN MONROE

Monroe was always comfortable in front of the camera — even on the beach.

Monroe as Evie in Dangerous Years (1947) — her first credited film appearance.

Monroe landed her first substantial role in the 1948 film Ladies of the Chorus.

The facts of her life have become legend, from her humble beginnings to her celebrated marriages to her mysterious death. Born Norma Jeane Mortensen on June 1, 1926, in Los Angeles to a mentally ill mother and absent father; she was christened Norma Jeane Baker. In her youth she shuttled between foster homes and orphanages when her mother was institutionalized. Desperate to create a "real" family of her own, she married James Dougherty at the age of sixteen. However, the marriage didn't last; youthful Norma Jeane was too restless to be content as a housewife.

"I want to be a big star more than anything," she once said. "It's something precious." The war years helped Monroe get started toward that goal. When her husband was assigned to overseas duty, she found work as a paint sprayer and parachute packer in an aircraft plant. In June 1945, photojournalist David Conover came to the plant to photograph women's contributions to the war effort. Monroe made the perfect subject, thus beginning her love affair with the camera.

With Conover's encouragement, she quit her job and pursued a modeling career. By the end of the year, Monroe had signed with the Emmaline Snively Modeling Agency and appeared on the cover of thirty-three major magazines. By then, however, her real goal was to be an actress. Intrigued by her photos, RKO head Howard Hughes was the first to offer her a screen test, but she declined and signed with 20th Century Fox for $125 a week.

About this time, she took her mother's maiden name and officially changed her first name to the more glamorous Marilyn. She cut her hair, bleached it blonde, and learned to smile with lips that quivered slightly. It was 1946 — and Marilyn Monroe was born.

All these changes weren't enough to get her billing in her first movie. Her bit part in the 1947 film *The Shocking Miss Pilgrim,* starring Betty Grable and Dick Haymes, went uncredited. That same year she won a small part in *Scudda Hoo! Scudda Hey!* but two of her three scenes wound up on the cutting room floor, leaving only a far-away shot of her in a canoe. In 1947, Monroe finally got credit for a small part in *Dangerous Years,* playing Evie, who works at a juke joint where the town's teen delinquents hang out. A low-budget film headlined by former "Dead End" kid Billy Halop, *Dangerous Years* disappeared soon after release.

As Monroe expanded her Hollywood connections, she began to develop her musical skills under the direction of Fred Karger. He helped her win the second lead in *Ladies of the Chorus,* in 1948, where she earned critical acclaim for her singing. Monroe plays Peggy, a chorus girl who falls in love with a wealthy young man. When the featured dancer leaves the show, Peggy takes her place. In spite of the obstacles, love triumphs — and so does Monroe. She sang, "Every Baby Needs a Da Da Daddy" and "Anyone Can Tell I Love You." A subsequent review in the Motion Picture Herald said, "One of the bright spots is Miss Monroe's singing … she shows promise."

In spite of the good reviews, the studio dropped her and she bounced from studio to studio appearing in small roles. Her career finally got a major jolt in 1950 with two showy roles in *The Asphalt Jungle* and *All About Eve*. As the luminously sexy aspiring actress Miss Caswell in the latter film, Monroe manages the difficult feat of holding her own opposite Bette Davis in full-diva mode and George Sanders at his most urbane. Stardom would come three years later with *Gentlemen Prefer Blondes* (1953). Throughout the fifties, she would star in a series of sex farces that defined the nation's attitudes, including *The Seven Year Itch* (1955), *Bus Stop* (1956), and *Some Like It Hot* (1959). Her impact as a cultural icon lives to this day.

"I want to be a big star more than anything. It's something precious."

— Marilyn Monroe

PAUL NEWMAN

Casting agents knew that his electric blue eyes and aquiline features had box office appeal.

Paul Newman captured the imagination of audiences and directors alike in the fifties with the authority and humanity he invested in his roles, no matter how flawed or unscrupulous the characters. Rather than play it safe in traditional romantic leads or heroic roles, Newman has consistently sought out fringe, misfit characters who don't readily engender audience sympathy, such as pool shark "Fast Eddie" Felson in *The Hustler* (1961) and the prodigal son of a Texas rancher in *Hud* (1963).

It was the skies, rather than the stage, that captured Newman's imagination while growing up in Depression-era Cleveland, Ohio. Born January 26, 1925, to the owner of a sporting goods store and his wife, Newman flirted with acting in grade school and high school, but his true aspiration was to become a naval pilot. Called up in 1943, Newman was crushed to learn that he was colorblind, and thus ineligible to fly. Instead, he spent three years working as a radio operator aboard a torpedo bomber in the South Pacific. When he was discharged, Newman enrolled in Ohio's Kenyon College, where he majored in English and started on the football team. Rowdy behavior soon got him kicked off the team, so he turned to acting — with stints in summer stock and the Chicago-based Woodside Players. His father's death in 1950, however, forced Newman to put aside his acting ambitions to run the family store. Ill-suited to the work, Newman rejoiced when the store was sold a year later. He went on to study at the Yale Drama School for a year and then left to join the throngs making the daily rounds of casting calls for acting jobs in New York City.

Within weeks, Newman won two walk-on parts on live television. His first role, as an old man applauding President McKinley in *The March of Time*, earned him $75. Within a few months he had secured a running part on *The Aldrich Family* for $200 a month. Around this time, Newman agreed to help an actress friend with her audition for membership in the prestigious Actor's Studio. They read a scene from Tennessee Williams's *Battle of Angels* in front of a large group. Those who passed were to perform a second audition before director Elia Kazan and producer Cheryl Crawford. To Newman's surprise, he was offered immediate membership while his friend was rejected.

In the fall of 1952, Newman's agent got him an audition for William Inge's new Broadway drama *Picnic*. He was initially cast as the sexy drifter Hal Carter, who tempts a rural Kansas beauty, but was later switched to the supporting role of Alan Seymour, a shy college boy who loses the girl. The play became a Pulitzer Prize-winning hit, running fourteen months and earning Newman a nomination as one of *Theatre World's* Promising Personalities of 1953.

On the strength of his performance, Newman was offered a five-year contract with Warner Brothers for $1,000 a week. The studio was then casting the role of Cal Trask in the film version of John Steinbeck's *East Of Eden*. Director Elia Kazan had narrowed the choices down to two young men from the Actor's Studio — Newman and James Dean. The legendary part went to Dean, leaving Newman free to make his feature debut in *The Silver Chalice* (1954), a religious epic he later called "the worst film made in the entirety of the 1950s."

In this epic, occasionally pretentious film, Newman plays Basil, a slave and silversmith who wears a toga and speaks in the stilted, arch dialogue that undermines so many historical dramas. Basil is commissioned to cast the Cup of Christ in silver and etch a design of the disciples around the edges. The movie was panned by critics and shunned by the public. Newman was so embarrassed by the film that when it was shown on TV many years later, he took out an ad in a Los Angeles newspaper, apologizing to viewers. Luckily, he got the chance to redeem himself in his next movie, *Somebody Up There Likes Me* (1956), the biography of boxing great Rocky Graziano.

Newman's debut role — as Basil in the forgettable epic The Silver Chalice *(1954).*

Newman's big break came two years after his film debut, as boxer Rocky Graziano in Somebody Up There Likes Me *(1956).*

JACK NICHOLSON

The unusual circumstances of Jack Nicholson's childhood have long been fodder for the tabloids. Born April 22, 1937 in Neptune, New Jersey, Nicholson grew up in his grandmother's care after his alcoholic father skipped town. His young mother remained a part of his life, but claimed to be an older sister, while Nicholson's grandmother pretended to be his birth mother. They maintained this elaborate ruse well into Nicholson's adulthood — he, in fact, only learned the truth when a magazine reporter examined his birth records.

Nicholson was restless from an early age. Neptune seemed parochial and confining, so at the age of seventeen, he jumped at the chance to visit relatives in California. He originally planned to return home for college, but the allure of Hollywood captured his imagination. To support himself, he accepted work as an errand boy at MGM. Meanwhile, he began studying with a local acting troupe called the Players Ring Theater.

At the age of 20, Nicholson signed with small-time agent Byron Griffith, who quickly arranged for him to appear in a few television commercials. But more substantial work still eluded him. When producer Roger Corman asked Griffith to suggest a few young actors for an upcoming low-budget thriller, Griffith submitted the name of one of his other clients, barely mentioning Nicholson's name. To Griffith's surprise, Corman chose Nicholson, preferring his edge to the other actor's unblemished good looks. At his screen test, Nicholson read the lead part — since none of the other parts had enough lines — even though a rising star named Tom Pittman had already been cast in the role. Corman's talent scout thought his reading was sensational, revealing a depth of character study unique for such a young actor. When Pittman's contract negotiations fell through, Corman and his crew wasted no time in casting Nicholson as the male lead in the film, called *The Cry Baby Killer* (1958).

Playing a slightly neurotic young hood who commits a crime of passion, Nicholson hits just the right notes, even with the B-movie script that left him little room to develop his role. Despite a few rough edges, Corman was satisfied enough to offer the young actor similar roles in 1960's *Too Soon to Love* and *The Wild Ride*. To Corman's credit, he recognized early that Nicholson's good looks had a sinister tilt that could be exploited in psychologically unstable characters. For nearly ten years, the two would be frequent collaborators on fringe films like *The Little Shop of Horrors* (1960) and *The Trip* (1967), a psychedelic film that Nicholson wrote.

In 1969, he finally escaped the confines of the B-movies when he replaced Rip Torn in the small role of an alcoholic lawyer in *Easy Rider*. His performance earned him a Best Supporting Actor nomination and the attention of the major studios. After a misstep as Barbra Streisand's hippy brother in the flop musical *On a Clear Day You Can See Forever* (1970), Nicholson achieved true stardom as the tortured concert pianist in Bob Rafelson's *Five Easy Pieces* (1970) — twelve years after his debut.

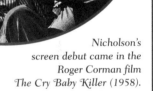

Nicholson's good looks had a sinister tilt that could be exploited in psychologically unstable characters.

Nicholson's screen debut came in the Roger Corman film The Cry Baby Killer (1958).

In 1969 Nicholson got his big break when Rip Torn bowed out of the role of George Hanson in Easy Rider, which also starred Peter Fonda (left) and Dennis Hopper (in background, left).

ROBERT REDFORD

Even in his early years the future heartthrob was much more than the sum of his blonde hair, chiseled features, and golden-boy charm.

Publicity still from War Hunt *(1962), Redford's big-screen debut.*

Redford (left) in action in a still from War Hunt.

Charles Robert Redford Jr. stumbled into acting when he lost interest in becoming a professional baseball player. Born August 18, 1937, in Santa Monica, California, Redford was an indifferent student whose misadventures included stealing hubcaps and scaling tall buildings to amuse himself. Even in his early years the future heartthrob was much more than the sum of his blonde hair, chiseled features, and golden-boy charm. From early on, he possessed his own brand of intelligence, sincerity, and athleticism, the latter being a catalyst in winning him many roles, including the Olympic hopeful in *Downhill Racer* (1969) and the nineteenth-century frontier recluse in *Jeremiah Johnson* (1972).

At the University of Colorado, sports seemed to dominate his attention. A gifted athlete, Redford went to Colorado on a baseball scholarship, but soon lost interest and flunked out of school. He then studied art at the Pratt Institute in New York, and left for Europe determined to become a fine artist. When he returned to New York, however, Redford abandoned his artistic aspirations to enroll in the American Academy of Dramatic Arts.

One of Redford's instructors was also a stage manager for the Broadway play *Tall Story.* In need of a few students for small roles in a crowd scene, he recruited Redford for the role of a college basketball player. Redford dribbled a basketball across the stage and spoke only one line, but still managed to make an impression on director Herman Shumlin. Still, no further work materialized, and Redford left New York for California to work in television.

Between 1960 and 1964, Redford appeared in over thirty television shows, including *Perry Mason, Alfred Hitchcock Presents, Route 66, Dr. Kildare,* and *The Twilight Zone.* His TV debut was on April 30, 1960, in an NBC drama called *The Deputy.* But it was his performance a month later in CBS's *Playhouse 90* that won rave reviews and considerable attention. The episode, "In the Presence of Mine Enemies," is about life in Nazi-occupied Poland during World War II. Redford plays a young Nazi officer trying to balance his personal values with his military duty. Though his performance had created a demand for his services, Redford turned down several offers and returned to New York to work in the theater. The daily grind of acting onstage wore him down, however, and he returned to Los Angeles to work in feature films.

In 1962, Redford made his film debut in the Korean War drama *War Hunt.* He portrays Private Roy Loomis, who has suspicions about a fellow soldier, Endore (John Saxon). When a cease-fire is called and Endore steals away with an eight-year-old war orphan, the squad must search for him. The movie was well-received by film critics and Redford was singled out for his moving performance. Although stardom was still years away for Redford, *War Hunt* was to have a lasting impact on his career.

He formed an enduring personal and professional bond with fellow cast member Sydney Pollack, who later became an accomplished director. Pollack has since cast Redford in a variety of heroic roles, as characters who distrust authority and prefer to rely on their own values. As a result, Redford has become one of the screen's most idealistic rebels, stubbornly maintaining his integrity — even in the face of overwhelming opposition. Pollack has directed Redford in seven films, including *The Way We Were* (1973) and *The Electric Horseman* (1979), which are considered by many to be Redford's best roles.

PETER SELLERS

Peter Sellers's first movie roles were in zany British comedies of the early fifties — perfomances that have rarely been seen in the United States. At that time it was assumed that English humor didn't translate well to American audiences. Like his fellow Englishman, Alec Guinness, Sellers vanishes into every role. His elusive presence reveals almost nothing of his true self. When he became known to American audiences in the early sixties, he was recognized for having a chameleon-like virtuosity, an ability few comedians of his era have ever matched.

Role-playing began early for Sellers, who was born Richard Henry Sellers on September 8, 1925, in Southsea, England. His entertainer parents called him Peter, after an older brother who had died at birth. He made his first stage appearance at an early age and spent most of his childhood in front of an audience. His parents were convinced that music and dancing — both of Sellers's parents were musical performers — were the keys to Sellers's future. He studied at two dance academies before beginning high school at St. Aloysius' School for Boys, where he learned to play several instruments and further developed his gift for mimicry.

Upon returning from Royal Air Force service in World War II, Sellers went on several radio auditions, but received no job offers. With characteristic bravado, he decided to circumvent the ordinary channels of talent recruitment. Impersonating one of BBC producer Roy Speer's performers, Sellers phoned Speer and suggested that an up-and-coming talent named Peter Sellers be cast in the popular program *Show Time*. Speer quickly discovered the ruse but enjoyed the daring of the prank so much that he gave the young actor a job.

This stroke of fortune would eventually pay off in the form of a television career. His talents as an impressionist and flair for improvisational comedy soon won Sellers a starring role in BBC's *The Goon Show*, a precursor to *Monty Python's Flying Circus*. The show's screwball antics got off to a slow start with audiences, but soon developed a sizeable following. More importantly, *The Goon Show*'s characters and gag routines became the basis of Sellers's first three movie outings.

The first of these was 1951's *Penny Points to Paradise*, in which Sellers reprised his popular radio character, the inept Major Bloodnok. Advanced Studios underwrote the venture, hoping to capitalize on the popularity of a proven franchise. The plot involves a bumbling group of counterfeiters who attempt to substitute their phony money for the winnings of a football betting pool. Various slapstick hijinks follow as the winning bettors attempt to safeguard their money.

Playing alongside his on-air cohorts Spike Milligan and Harry Secombe, Sellers displays his substantial comic talent, but his performance is uneven, largely due to the mediocre material. Despite its weak script, the film achieved moderate commercial success, and two more *Goon Show* takeoffs followed — *Down Among the Z Men*, in 1952 and *The Goon Movie*, in 1953. On the strength of these performances, Sellers was cast in an increasingly desirable string of film roles, though he remained with *The Goon Show* until its cancellation in 1960.

In 1963, Sellers appeared for the first time as Inspector Clouseau in *The Pink Panther*. Oblivious to the comic anarchy he creates, the earnest and monumentally inept Clouseau won Sellers admirers the world over. He appeared in five sequels, the last of which was created from footage leftover after his untimely death of a heart attack in 1980.

Sellers as Tully Bascombe in the first film that won him recognition in the United States, The Mouse That Roared (1959).

Sellers was recognized for having a chameleon-like virtuosity, an ability few comedians have ever matched.

A more portly Sellers in one of his earlier films, Orders are Orders (1954).

BARBRA STREISAND

Before she appeared in her first film, Streisand was given her own TV special, My Name is Barbra (1965).

Streisand's first movie role as Fanny Brice in Funny Girl (1968) reprised her role from the Broadway production.

Barbra Streisand's journey from a Brooklyn apartment to Hollywood stardom eventually earned her Oscar, Emmy, Grammy, and Tony Awards. When she began her career in the early sixties, cookie-cutter beauty and a white bread, mainstream sensibility were the rule in Hollywood. But Streisand was Jewish, very much a New Yorker, and proudly bore features uncommon in leading ladies, though many patrons of the Broadway theater where she began her performing career found her attractive, albeit unconventionally.

Born April 24, 1942, she grew up under the critical eye of her mother, who demanded that she always do her best. Streisand's father had died when she was a toddler. Although an honors student at Erasmus High School, Streisand was more interested in performing than in academics. With no support or encouragement from home, she entered and won a talent contest at The Lion, a small club in Greenwich Village. Soon she attracted a following at the several area clubs where she performed.

Graduating from high school two years early, Barbara dropped the middle "a" from her name and worked as a waitress and switchboard operator while continuing to perform whenever she could. In 1961, she won a role in an off-Broadway play, which closed after only one night. The following year, Streisand made it to Broadway with a supporting role in the musical *I Can Get It for You Wholesale*. The show lasted only nine months, but Streisand's scene-stealing performance as the beleaguered secretary Miss Marmelstein brought her a Tony nomination. She also signed her first recording contract with Columbia Records that year. When *The Barbra Streisand Album* came out in 1963, it sold more than a million copies and won her Grammies for Best Female Vocalist and Best Album of the Year.

Broadway came calling again with a part made to order for Streisand: Ziegfeld Girl and comedienne Fanny Brice. A musical version of Brice's life called *Funny Girl* was then in rehearsals with Anne Bancroft, but Bancroft lacked the vocal range for the part and left the show. Streisand happily stepped into the role and gave a star-making performance that brought her a second Tony nomination. Although she lost to Carol Channing of *Hello, Dolly!* she later won an honorary Tony for her stage work.

Having conquered stage and recording, Streisand next turned her attention to television. She signed a 10-year contract with CBS Television to produce and star in TV specials for the network. In an unprecedented move, they also gave her complete artistic control — and they weren't disappointed. Her first TV special, *My Name is Barbra*, won five Emmy Awards.

The big screen was all that remained. When Columbia Pictures decided to make a film version of *Funny Girl* in 1968, it was understood that Streisand would reprise her stage role. Critics speculated she would merely be recycling her winning stage performance, but under William Wyler's direction, Streisand effortlessly recreated her role without excessive theatrics. She captured both the broad humor and pathos that set Brice apart from most of Ziegfeld's stars. A critical and commercial blockbuster, *Funny Girl* was one of the last of the big-budget sixties musicals to turn a profit. Streisand's performance brought her the coveted Oscar in a landmark tie with Katharine Hepburn, who was nominated for *The Lion in Winter*. She had achieved true movie stardom.

MODERN MUSICAL STARS

In the late fifties and sixties, filmmakers turned increasingly to the Broadway stage for musical material, rather than creating original works for the screen. While some musicals — like *West Side Story* (1961) and *The Sound of Music* (1965) — scored both critically and commercially, the genre began to self-destruct with a series of overblown and over-budget films in the late sixties. A new sound, rock and roll, hit the big screen in the fifties, though only a handful of rock stars have ever achieved genuine crossover stardom in movies. These singers all debuted in films during this time.

Julie Andrews, born Julia Elizabeth Wells to music hall performers, was a brilliant child singer who made her London stage debut at the age of twelve. She eventually made it to Broadway, starring opposite Rex Harrison in *My Fair Lady,* and then to Hollywood, debuting and starring in the Disney film, *Mary Poppins* (1964), for which she won an Oscar. Although this was Andrews's onscreen debut, the singer's voice had debuted in the 1949 animated film, *La Rosa di Bagdad*. A throwback to an earlier era, the wholesome, cheerful Andrews became a major box office star in *The Sound of Music* (1965) and *Thoroughly Modern Millie* (1967).

Cher, born Cherilyn Sarkisian LaPiere, was a singing star when she landed her first dramatic film role in *Chastity* (1969), written by husband Sonny Bono. The duo embarked on a very successful television career in 1971 with *The Sonny and Cher Comedy Hour.* It wouldn't be until the 1980s, however, that Cher would break out as a talented and mature actress in *Silkwood* (1983) and *Moonstruck* (1987), which won her a much-coveted Academy Award.

Elvis Presley was already hailed as the "King of Rock and Roll" when he confided to a *Newsweek* reporter that he wanted to be a dramatic actor in 1956. Despite his lack of experience, 20th Century Fox rushed the Tupelo, Mississippi, native into his first starring role, the Civil War-era western, *Love Me Tender* (1956). As the second lead to B-movie stalwart Richard Egan and starlet Debra Paget, Presley gets the chance to perform both an incongruous musical number set at a county fair and the title song. Critics were unimpressed, but the film was a huge success. Presley went on to make thirty more films that, for the most part, adhere closely to a formula: narrative and character development are simply filler between his hip-swiveling musical numbers.

Julie Andrews (top), Cher (bottom)

(facing page) Elvis Presley

ON- AND OFF-BROADWAY

The theater has long been the proving ground for aspiring actors and actresses. Here are a few of the actors of the fifties and sixties who parlayed successful stage work into film stardom.

Anne Bancroft, born Anna Maria Louise Italiano, made her film debut in 1952 in *Don't Bother to Knock.* She went on to appear in several B-films before deciding to return to the stage. It was on Broadway that she made a name for herself, starring with Henry Fonda in the 1958 production of *Two for the Seesaw,* for which she won a Tony Award. The next year she won her second Tony for her performance as Helen Keller's teacher and mentor, Annie Sullivan, in *The Miracle Worker.* She became a film star after recreating this role in the 1962 film version of the play, which won her the Academy Award for Best Actress.

Faye Dunaway, the daughter of an Army officer, grew up traveling the world. After college, she worked with the Lincoln Center Repertory Company before appearing off-Broadway in *Hogan's Goat.* This play led to her screen debut in *The Happening* in 1967. It was another movie released a few months after her debut, however, which launched Dunaway into stardom — *Bonnie and Clyde,* with Warren Beatty. Her intense, sexually charged performance as Depression-era gun moll Bonnie Parker brought Dunaway her first Oscar nomination. She would later win the Oscar for *Network* (1976).

Robert Duvall started acting at New York's Neighborhood Playhouse after fighting in the Korean War. He made his film debut as the mysterious neighbor Boo Radley in the classic coming-of-age drama *To Kill a Mockingbird* (1962). The consummate character actor, Duvall continued working steadily through the sixties before taking on his breakthrough role as the Corleone family advisor, Tom Hagen, in *The Godfather* (1972), which earned him an Oscar nomination for Best Supporting Actor.

Gene Hackman, was a late bloomer who got his acting start in his early 30s, after serving for three years in the Marines. After trying his hand at several different professions, he decided to become an actor, joining the Pasadena Playhouse. His work there eventually took him to Broadway, where he starred in the hit play, *Any Wednesday.* In 1961, Hackman made his big-screen debut in the low-budget crime thriller, *Mad Dog Coll.* Three years later, he won a meaty supporting role in the psychological drama, *Lilith* (1964). More supporting roles followed until 1971's *The French Connection,* which brought Hackman an Oscar for his breakout performance as New York police detective "Popeye" Doyle.

Sidney Poitier, the son of a dirt farmer, was born in Miami, Florida, but grew up in the Bahamas. After serving in the Army, he joined the American Negro Theater and, in 1946, made his Broadway debut. His big-screen debut was in *No Way Out* (1950). Poitier made Hollywood history in 1963 by becoming the first African-American actor to win the Oscar for Best Actor, for *Lilies of the Field.*

Jason Robards Jr., the son of the accomplished stage actor Jason Robards, started his acting career in New York, after serving seven years in the Navy and surviving the Pearl Harbor attack. After the war he worked on the stage, and by the time he made his big-screen debut in the 1959 film, *The Journey,* he was already an accomplished Broadway star, most notably for his work in the plays of Eugene O'Neill. His screen career was just as successful as his stage career — Robards won Oscars for *All the President's Men* (1976) and *Julia* (1977).

(top to bottom) Anne Bancroft, Faye Dunaway, Robert Duvall, Gene Hackman, Sidney Poitier, and Jason Robards Jr.

THE RAT PACK

Although they appeared in only a few films, most notably *Oceans Eleven* (1960), the group of actors known as the "Rat Pack" set the standard for cool in the late fifties and early sixties. Led by Frank Sinatra, these Las Vegas entertainers and full-time playboys became notorious for their womanizing and reported connections to an unsavory crowd. Forty years later, the Rat Pack continues to inspire would-be hipsters.

Joey Bishop   *Sammy Davis Jr.*   *Peter Lawford*   *Dean Martin*

Frank Sinatra, a saloon singer from Hoboken, New Jersey, virtually disappeared from the big screen in the late forties and early fifties. The resilient crooner and actor would return, however — he won an Academy Award for Best Supporting Actor as the ill-fated Maggio in *From Here to Eternity* (1953).

Joey Bishop was born Joseph Abraham Gottlieb in the Bronx in 1918. His family moved to South Philadelphia, where Bishop got his start in the entertainment business, forming the Bishop Brothers Trio. World War II forced Bishop to put his career on hold, however, and it wasn't until he befriended Sinatra that Bishop's career finally got back on track. In 1957, Bishop appeared in his first film, *The Deep Six*. He subsequently appeared with the Rat Pack in *Oceans Eleven* (1960) and *Sergeants 3* (1962).

Sammy Davis Jr. began his career at three in the family vaudeville act. In 1933, at the age of five, Davis appeared with Ethel Waters in his first film, *Rufus Jones for President*. In this short, Davis sings and tap dances his way into the White House. As an adult, he finally emerged as a popular recording artist and Hollywood movie star. A dedicated member of the Rat Pack, Davis was also probably the group's most versatile entertainer, and an extremely talented singer, dancer, actor, and comedian.

Peter Lawford, the son of a knighted World War I British general, landed his first big-screen role in the 1930 British film, *Poor Old Bill*, when he was just eight. He later traveled to Hollywood where he would eventually star in a handful of popular romantic roles, including the musicals *Good News* (1947) and *Royal Wedding* (1951). He soon hooked up with Frank Sinatra and his crowd and married into the Kennedy family. The debonair Lawford, a bona fide member of the Rat Pack, went on to star in *Sergeants 3* (1962) and team with Sammy Davis Jr. in the comedy *Salt and Pepper* (1968).

Dean Martin, born Dino Paul Crocetti, was a boxer who got his start in the entertainment business as a nightclub singer. His travels brought him in touch with comedian Jerry Lewis in 1946, and the two partnered to become one of the most popular comedy teams of all time. Three years later, the successful duo took their act to the big screen in the 1949 film, *My Friend Irma*. In addition to his films with the Rat Pack, Martin stretched his talents in films ranging from war dramas like *The Young Lions* (1958) to the tongue-in-cheek Matt Helm spy movies of the sixties.

Frank Sinatra

OTHER STARS OF THE PERIOD

Brigitte Bardot took up dancing as a young child. By the time she was fifteen, she appeared on the cover of the French magazine, *Elle*. The photo attracted national attention and in 1952 she was cast in her first film, *Le Trou Normand (Crazy for Love)*. In 1954, Bardot had a small part in her first American film, *An Act of Love*, with Kirk Douglas. She continued making movies in France, however. In 1956 she starred for her director husband Roger Vadim in *...And God Created Woman*, a film that shocked many with its frank sexuality and Bardot's brief nude scene. A sexual provocateur, Bardot (known as BB to her fans) became an international sensation. She was extremely popular in the United States, where she graced the cover of countless magazines and her films attracted eager audiences.

Warren Beatty followed in the acting footsteps of older sister Shirley MacLaine. He started on Broadway and in television's *The Many Loves of Dobie Gillis* before making an auspicious debut opposite Natalie Wood in 1961's *Splendor in the Grass*. Known for his offscreen exploits with his costars, Beatty is also an acclaimed writer, director, and producer. In 1978, he made his directing debut in *Heaven Can Wait*, in which he also starred. He was nominated for an Academy Award as both actor and director. He won a Best Director Oscar three years later for *Reds* (1981).

Jane Fonda was a restless Vassar graduate (first wanting to be an artist and then a model), but she eventually followed in her father Henry's footsteps after meeting the legendary acting teacher Lee Strasberg. She appeared on Broadway soon after and, in 1960, made her film debut in the comedy, *Tall Story*. She worked steadily in the sixties, earning both acclaim and notoriety, alternating serious drama with kitsch-films like *Barbarella* (1968). In 1969 she was nominated for an Oscar for her performance in *They Shoot Horses, Don't They?* She won the Oscar two years later for *Klute* (1971), and again in 1978 for *Coming Home*.

Goldie Hawn, who achieved stardom as an accomplished comedic actor, actually got her start as a can-can dancer at the 1964 World's Fair in New York. Later, she became a go-go dancer, but in 1968, Hawn finally got her big break as a regular on the television comedy series *Rowan & Martin's Laugh-In*. After a doing little more than a few giggles as a walk-on in *The One and Only, Genuine, Original Family Band* (1968), Hawn made her acting debut in the plum role of Walter Matthau's kooky mistress in *Cactus Flower* (1969) and won the Academy Award for Best Supporting Actress.

Jane Fonda

Brigitte Bardot   Warren Beatty   Goldie Hawn   Charlton Heston

Charlton Heston was born Charles Carter in Evanston, Illinois, in 1924. He studied drama at Northwestern University and, while still a student, appeared in the student-produced 1941 film, *Peer Gynt.* After serving three years in the Air Force, he returned to civilian life and began acting in earnest, appearing on Broadway and in numerous television productions. He also appeared in another amateur film before finally landing a starring role in the feature film, *Dark City* (1950). Nine years later, he won an Academy Award for his performance in *Ben-Hur* (1959).

Walter Matthau was born Walter Matuschanskavasky to Russian-Jewish immigrants on the Lower East Side of New York City. As a kid, he peddled sodas at a Yiddish theater, but soon he was performing on the stage. After high school, Matthau entered the Army Air Corps, in which he served during World War II. When he returned, he enrolled in the New School's dramatic workshop; shortly after, he made his debut on Broadway. In 1955, Matthau made his first big-screen appearance in *The Kentuckian,* and, just a decade later, he was awarded an Oscar for his role in the 1966 film, *The Fortune Cookie,* the first of many collaborations with Jack Lemmon.

Shirley MacLaine's love for dance began at the tender age of two. After high school, she moved to New York to pursue a dance career. She landed parts in several Broadway shows and was Carol Haney's understudy for *The Pajama Game* in 1954. When Haney broke her leg, MacLaine went on as the show's female lead. Film producer Hal Wallis caught the show and signed her to a movie contract. Her film debut came in Alfred Hitchcock's black comedy, *The Trouble with Harry,* in 1955. Nominated five times for Best Actress, she won the Academy Award for 1983's *Terms of Endearment.*

Steve McQueen drew on a variety of life experiences in his acting. He was a lumberjack, sailor, carnival barker, bartender, and beachcomber before he studied acting in New York. In 1955 he got his first break, replacing Ben Gazzara in *A Hatful of Rain* on Broadway. His film debut came the next year with a bit part in *Somebody Up There Likes Me.* Two years later he won his first lead role in the drive-in teen classic, *The Blob.* He gained popularity for his television role in *Wanted: Dead or Alive,* but continued to work in films as well. True film stardom came with his performance as a daring World War II American prisoner of war in *The Great Escape* (1963). McQueen was nominated for an Academy Award for his performance in *The Sand Pebbles* in 1966.

Kim Novak worked as an elevator operator, dime-store salesgirl, dental assistant and appliance spokesmodel before breaking into movies. Columbia contracted with her in 1954, hoping that she would be their answer to Marilyn Monroe. That year, the studio used her as an uncredited extra in *The French Line* and a few months later cast her in her first movie role, in *Pushover,* opposite Fred MacMurray. *Five Against the House* and *The Man With the Golden Arm* followed in 1955, before she became a household name later that year with her performance in *Picnic.* By the end of 1955 she was a top box office draw, but her popularity declined in the early 1960s.

Anthony Quinn was born Antonio Quinones in Mexico in 1916. Moving to Los Angeles with his family when he was young, he worked a variety of jobs, ranging from boxer to preacher, before finally turning to acting. After a few parts on the local stage, he landed a small non-speaking role in *Parole* in 1936, and followed it up later in the year with the role of an Indian warrior in *The Plainsman.* He eventually became one of the best-known character actors in the history of Hollywood, winning two Academy Awards for Best Supporting Actor for *Viva Zapata!* in 1952 and *Lust for Life* in 1956.

Walter Matthau   Shirley MacLaine   Steve McQueen   Anthony Quinn

1970-PRESENT

Steven Spielberg became a household name with Jaws *(1975), starring Roy Scheider, Robert Shaw, and Richard Dreyfuss.*

Television's Saturday Night Live *emerged in 1975 to gradually change the face of comedy in the movies.*

CONTEMPORARY CINEMA

The early seventies found America demoralized. The promise of the "Age of Aquarius" had dissipated, as the Vietnam War raged on with no end in sight. Rampant inflation and the energy crisis took a toll on the national morale, which plunged even lower following Nixon's Watergate scandal.

Early seventies cinema reflects this disillusionment and cynicism. Stark, gritty filmmaking came into vogue with graphic violence, sexuality, and profanity becoming commonplace. As a consequence, the Motion Picture Association of America introduced a rating system for films.

A new breed of young directors appeared early in the decade to revitalize American cinema. Francis Ford Coppola's *The Godfather* (1972) revived the gangster genre while Steven Spielberg's *Jaws* (1975) terrified audiences and emptied the nation's beaches.

The worldwide success of *Jaws* was later eclipsed by George Lucas's space fantasy, *Star Wars* (1977). A high-tech homage to both Flash Gordon serials and westerns, *Star Wars* became the top grossing film of all time. Both *Jaws* and *Star Wars* set the pattern for future summer blockbusters: big-budget, effects-driven spectacles released simultaneously to thousands of theaters nationwide.

While summer blockbusters may have generated huge revenues for the studios, they were particularly disheartening for actresses, who had already spent most of the decade scrambling for decent roles. Except for Barbra Streisand and Jane Fonda, most female stars were reduced to playing the hero's girlfriend. Only Streisand consistently drew audiences to the same degree as box office magnets Clint Eastwood, Burt Reynolds, and Robert Redford.

The emphasis on the financial bottom line carried over into the eighties. Extolling the virtues of fiscal and social conservatism, actor-turned-politician Ronald Reagan was elected President by a landslide in 1980. During his presidency, the country's economy rebounded from the recession of the seventies. Yuppies became conspicuous consumers, racking up debt to finance their homes, cars, and vacations. Many took Michael Douglas's words in *Wall Street* (1987) as their credo: "greed is good."

Hollywood rode this economic boom, despite competition from cable television and video. Cinema strongmen Arnold Schwarzenegger and Sylvester Stallone became superstars in a series of testosterone-fueled hit-action films.

Obi-Wan Kenobi battles Darth Vader in George Lucas's epic, Star Wars (1977).

Matthew Broderick starred in the title role of Ferris Bueller's Day Off (1986).

Teen movies and comedies were the other staples of eighties cinema. Young stars like Molly Ringwald and Matthew Broderick appeared in such hit films as *Sixteen Candles* (1984) and *Ferris Bueller's Day Off* (1986), both from director John Hughes. The new stars of comedy came mostly from television, particularly the long-running variety show, *Saturday Night Live*. Chevy Chase and John Belushi were the first of the show's cast members to cross over into movies; they were followed by Eddie Murphy, Bill Murray, Billy Crystal, and many others. Audiences seeking sophisticated, literate comedy turned to Woody Allen, who directed, wrote and starred in such acclaimed films as *Zelig* (1983) and *Hannah and Her Sisters* (1986).

As the nineties began, it was pretty much business as usual in Hollywood. Star salaries and budgets continued to climb, making it next to impossible to produce a studio film for anything less than $20 to $30 million. With so much money at stake, the studios did everything they could to diminish the potential for economic ruin. Paramount and 20th Century Fox jointly produced James Cameron's $200 million epic, *Titanic* (1997), which swept the Academy Awards and became the top grossing film of all time.

"Has-been" John Travolta reemerges in Pulp Fiction (1994), which grossed over $100 million.

Audience tastes proved ever fickle in the nineties. Former box office champions Schwarzenegger and Stallone gradually faded as audiences lost interest in their particular brand of action film. Harrison Ford, Tom Hanks, Mel Gibson, and Tom Cruise regularly drew audiences, as did female stars Julia Roberts, Meg Ryan, Jodie Foster, and Sandra Bullock. Unlike stars of the thirties, they were not subject to the dictates of studio bosses. Many set up their own companies to develop and produce films.

As always, there was no guarantee of what would hit or miss with audiences. In 1999, a low-budget, independent film shot on digital video literally came out of nowhere to gross over $100 million. The astonishing success of *The Blair Witch Project* sent a mini-shockwave through Hollywood. It appeared that any aspiring filmmaker could achieve what many veteran directors had pursued for many years. Only time will tell what this revelation ultimately means for Hollywood in the 21st century.

Titanic (1997), starring Leonardo DiCaprio, became the top grossing film of all time.

TOM CRUISE

Cruise as a teenager.

Cruise appeared in his first two films in 1981, Endless Love (his debut), and Taps (pictured above).

An ambitious, intense actor, Tom Cruise seems to relish the chance to upset expectations. Unlike some of his successful contemporaries, Cruise has distinguished himself by accepting challenging roles rather than coasting through formulaic star vehicles that require nothing more than his ample charm and charisma. Consistently seeking out provocative and controversial material, he has earned three Oscar nominations. His shrewd choices of commercial yet offbeat roles have proven that he is both a pop culture icon and a resourceful actor.

Cruise's early years are characterized by constant upheaval. Born Thomas Cruise Mapother IV on July 3, 1962, in Syracuse, New York, to an electrical engineer and a teacher, Cruise moved seven times before his eleventh birthday. His father's search for work led the family to crisscross the Eastern seaboard; as a result, Cruise was rarely in one place long enough to form any lasting friendships. Like many actors, his childhood experiences taught him to adapt quickly to new surroundings and different cultures.

Following his parents' divorce and his mother's subsequent remarriage, Cruise moved with his mother and stepfather to Basking Ridge, New Jersey. He was an accomplished athlete, but when a knee injury forced him to give up wrestling, Cruise turned to acting. Due to his dyslexia, school had long been a torturous experience for Cruise, whose mother patiently taught him how to focus and learn visually by employing his imagination instead of just reading words. With the drive that has characterized his film career, Cruise won the lead in a high school production of *Guys and Dolls*. His acting success gave him a newfound sense of accomplishment. When an agent saw the play and urged Cruise to pursue acting, he dropped his hard-to-pronounce surname, skipped his high school graduation, and moved to New York.

Cruise soon learned to live on a meager diet of hot dogs and rice, while auditioning and taking night classes to hone his craft. He endured his share of rejection, often for being either thought too intense or not handsome enough. Passed over for a role on the television series *Fame*, Cruise happily rebounded from this disappointment to win his first film role in the movie *Endless Love* (1981).

Based on the novel by Scott Spencer, *Endless Love* was produced to launch Brooke Shields as a full-fledged movie star. Cruise was oblivious to director Franco Zefferelli's fame when he auditioned. He later admitted his ignorance was a blessing; he would have been far too nervous if he had known he was reading in front of such a powerful man.

In this teen romance, Cruise plays Billy, a high school student who becomes a close friend of the lead character, David. Billy's cheerful and outgoing personality masks a secret he comes to share with his friend. He explains how he set fire to his neighbor's house when he was eight and then accepted a hero's praise when he alerted them to the blaze. For once, Cruise's intensity was deemed an asset, not a liability. The contrast between his

wholesome, high school jock façade and egocentric, amoral behavior is both unnerving and wholly plausible. Listed eighteenth in the credits, Cruise is onscreen for approximately seven minutes. As the press focused on Shields and her co-star Martin Hewitt, Cruise barely caused a ripple with his film debut. In retrospect, this was probably a good thing, since *Endless Love* opened to almost uniformly negative reviews and was middling at the box office. Cruise soon took on a larger role in the military school drama, *Taps* (1981), and later found his breakthrough role in the sleeper, *Risky Business* (1983).

> **"I give it everything, that's why I work so hard. I always tell young actors to take charge."**
> — Tom Cruise

ROBERT DE NIRO

From early on, Robert De Niro has consistently revealed the depth and sensitivity of characters once treated as monolithic bad guys — from Vito Corleone in *The Godfather, Part II* (1974) to Travis Bickle in *Taxi Driver* (1976) to Jake La Motta in *Raging Bull* (1980). But it would be inaccurate to pigeonhole De Niro as a master of violence and pent-up rage. What most distinguishes the man whom many call the greatest actor of his generation is his ability to disappear into a role, be it sympathetic or psychotic. De Niro's transformation in his screen roles is often so complete that fellow actors claim not to recognize him from one project to another

A painfully shy child who buried himself in books, De Niro was born on August 17, 1943, to artists in New York's Little Italy neighborhood. It was acting that gave De Niro the chance to overcome his shyness. More importantly, it also gave him a sense of purpose that has allowed him to fulfill his potential, since at the age of sixteen he was showing signs of becoming a small-time hoodlum. He left behind a life of petty crime from the time he made his stage debut in a production of Anton Chekhov's *The Bear.*

De Niro spent the next fifteen years paying his dues in small, off-Broadway stage productions. During this time, he studied at the Stella Adler Conservatory, where he learned Method acting techniques from the foremost authorities, including pioneers Lee Strasberg and Stella Adler. It would be many years, however, before De Niro came into his own as a Method actor. In the meantime, he had impressed actress Shelley Winters enough that she took him under her wing, providing him lodging at her apartment while he completed his studies.

At the age of twenty, four years into his fledgling stage career, De Niro landed his first role in a feature film. The project — an unmemorable, mostly formulaic comedy — was titled *The Wedding Party* (1969) and was the chief result of director Brian De Palma's graduate study at Sarah Lawrence College. De Palma is sometimes credited with discovering Robert De Niro, but in 1963, De Palma was as much a screen novice as De Niro was.

In *The Wedding Party,* De Niro plays Cecil, a friend of a cold-footed groom. Cecil first tries to convince the groom not to get married, but abruptly changes his mind in the middle of the movie, when he begins to counsel in favor of marriage. Although he has a major speaking part, De Niro's performance is almost as forgettable as Cecil's nondescript clothing and conservative haircut. His residual boyhood shyness comes through as De Niro seems to retreat from the camera, even in his speaking scenes.

The Wedding Party was poorly received, and its release was delayed until 1969, six years after its production. De Niro next starred in De Palma's *Greetings* (1968), which was the hit of the 1969 Berlin Film Festival. In this hard-edged satire of the late sixties' counterculture, De Niro plays Jon Rubin, a hippie draft dodger trying to keep his best friend out of the army. Although the X-rated film received little attention in the mainstream American press, De Niro's bold, inventive performance secured him steady work in films ranging from Roger Corman's *Bloody Momma* (1970) to Martin Scorsese's acclaimed *Mean Streets* (1973). Stardom and a Best Supporting Actor Academy Award would come with Francis Ford Coppola's *The Godfather, Part II.*

"It's important not to indicate. People don't try to show their feelings, they try to hide them."

— Robert De Niro, on his acting style

De Niro, in his first motion picture released in the United States — the Brian De Palma film *Greetings* (1968).

De Niro's big break came in 1973 with his part in *Bang the Drum Slowly,* in which he was cast with Vincent Gardenia (far right).

HARRISON FORD

Ford with fellow cast member Camilla Sparv in his first movie role as a bellhop in Dead Heat on a Merry-Go-Round (1966).

A few years after his solid performance in George Lucas's American Graffiti (1973), Lucas cast him in his breakthrough role as Han Solo in Star Wars (1977).

The son of an Irish father and Russian-Jewish mother, Harrison Ford has starred in four of the ten highest-grossing films of all time. Unlike many action stars, Ford brings a refreshing humanity and disarming wit to his roles.

Born July 13, 1942, in a Chicago suburb, Ford experienced an uneventful childhood and adolescence. A lackluster student, he enrolled in Spencer Tracy's alma mater, Ripon College in central Wisconsin, to study English and philosophy, but academics were overshadowed by his growing interest in acting. After quitting Ripon a month before graduation, Ford performed in summer stock theater and then headed west to Hollywood and the lure of a film career.

He started small — the Laguna Playhouse— and gradually worked his way up to better venues. A scout from Columbia's New Talent program was impressed with his performance in *John Brown's Body* and invited him to audition. It was an intimidating environment; without even meeting with him, studio executives took his name and number and showed him the door. Fate may have played a part in what happened next. On his way out, Ford decided to stop in the restroom. When he emerged, a studio employee was waiting with a contract for $150 a week.

Though it was a dream come true for a young actor in 1964, movie roles were still hard to come by, and Ford spent his days attending acting class. Meanwhile, he had purchased a house that needed some work. Borrowing books from the local library, he discovered that he was not only skilled in carpentry, but that he also enjoyed it. Over the next few years it was a skill that he would need.

After eighteen months with Columbia, Ford was assigned his first film role. It was only one day's work as a bellboy in the 1966 movie *Dead Heat on a Merry-Go-Round*. James Coburn stars as a con man in this comedy about a bank heist at the Los Angeles airport. As studio executives still felt that he was a limited talent, they gave him only a two-line part. They sent him back to acting classes, to be summoned a year later for two more unremarkable roles.

The first was a part in the 1967 film *Luv*, starring Jack Lemmon. The film got poor reviews, but that didn't affect Ford, who was not even listed in the credits. Later that year, he was cast as Lieutenant Shaffer in *A Time for Killing* (1967), a low-budget western set during the Civil War. Even though Columbia executives were duly impressed by Ford's performance in this small role, the studio dropped him from its list of contract players. Signed by Universal three days later, he made regular guest appearances on such television series as *Gunsmoke, The Virginian,* and *Ironside,* but a feature film lead still eluded him. In 1970, Ford decided that until he got the part he wanted, he was going to focus exclusively on carpentry.

In 1972, Ford auditioned for the George Lucas film, *American Graffiti*. Fred Roos, a friend from their days together at Columbia, was casting director. He was to audition a group of unknown actors for the ensemble cast and Ford made the cut — landing the role of hot rod driver Bob Falfa. A surprise hit, *American Graffiti* (1973) was the first of many lucrative collaborations between Lucas and Ford. As a result, Ford would put away his carpentry tools for good when *Star Wars* (1977) became a worldwide phenomenon.

> **"I don't use any particular method. I'm from the let's pretend school of acting."**
>
> — Harrison Ford

MEL GIBSON

The sixth of eleven children, Mel Columeille Gerard Gibson was born in Peekskill, New York, on January 3, 1956, to a New York Central Railroad brakeman and a former Australian opera singer. When his father was injured in 1968 on the job, he took his workers' compensation settlement and $21,000 in winnings from an appearance on the game show *Jeopardy* and moved the family to Australia. The Vietnam War was raging and Gibson's father wanted to protect his sons from the draft.

In the seventies, Australian cinema gained worldwide recognition. Australian filmmakers Peter Weir, Fred Schepisi, and Gillian Armstrong, among others, produced visually arresting and provocative films of international acclaim, such as *Picnic at Hanging Rock* (1975) and *The Chant of Jimmie Blacksmith* (1978). The directors from Down Under eventually made their way to Hollywood, as did the adoptive Aussie, Gibson, who would eventually benefit from Hollywood's eagerness to capitalize on the phenomenon.

But long before Hollywood's enchantment with Australia became a mania, Gibson had a long way to go before gaining acceptance from his new countrymen. In the late sixties, the young American transplant was teased by his classmates for his American accent. Defensively, he quickly acquired an Australian accent. The son of devout Irish Catholics, Gibson attended a Catholic high school and briefly considered becoming a chef or journalist when he graduated. When the time came, however, he was working at an orange juice factory with no real goals in mind. His sister Mary decided to help him find a direction. Recognizing his talent, she submitted his application to the National Institute of Dramatic Arts. Once accepted into the program, Gibson embarked on a new career, though he initially suffered from paralyzing stage fright.

While still a student, Gibson and his friend Steve Bisby landed their first film roles in producer Phil Avalon's low-budget surfing film *Summer City* (1977). As the carefree and irresponsible surfer Scollop, Gibson sports both long bleached blonde hair and a few extra pounds. His character's sole purpose is to find the perfect wave and a girlfriend. A less-than-memorable film, *Summer City* scarcely played in theaters in Australia and received practically no exposure in the U.S.

Still unknown to American audiences, in 1979 Gibson made two wildly different films. As the title character in *Tim,* he plays a simple-minded young man who falls in love with an older American woman (Piper Laurie). Based on the Colleen McCullough novel, *Tim* earned Gibson a "Sammy," the Australian equivalent of the Oscar. It was the second film, however, that ultimately led to Gibson's recognition in Hollywood. His voice teacher recommended that he audition for a role in *Mad Max,* a violent science fiction movie set in post-nuclear holocaust Australia. A bar fight before the audition left Gibson in bad shape — with a swollen face, broken nose, and stitches. Director George Miller took one look at his battered face and proclaimed him perfect for the role of Mad Max Rockatansky, an outcast action hero. Gibson had found his star vehicle.

His matinee-idol good looks hidden by bruises, Gibson gives an intensely felt, physical performance as a man driven to violence by loss, conveying Max's anguish primarily with minimal gestures. This role set the template for many of his future screen heroes, who often seek retribution through violence, but only after exhausting alternate measures. Although Gibson has dabbled in comedy, most recently in *What Women Want* (2000), he is best known for playing wounded, obsessive heroes haunted by private demons.

Gibson in Mad Max (1979) was cast as a violent outcast in a post-nuclear holocaust Australia.

A bar fight before the audition left Gibson in bad shape — with a swollen face, broken nose, and stitches. Director George Miller took one look at his battered face and proclaimed him perfect for the role of Mad Max.

Mad Max proved to be Gibson's star vehicle. He also starred in the film's two sequels.

TOM HANKS

Hanks's first national exposure was in a starring role in the hit TV sitcom Bosom Buddies *(1980), in which he and Peter Scolari played men masquerading as women.*

Four years after his film debut in a forgettable horror movie, Hanks's career took off with a role in the hit movie Splash *(1984), in which he starred with Daryl Hannah.*

An engaging, witty actor with extraordinary range, Tom Hanks wears his stardom with a minimum of theatrics and ostentation — even when his characters endure an emotional meltdown. Like James Stewart, to whom he is often compared, Hanks has an uncanny ability to appear both refreshingly normal and larger-than-life onscreen. Like Stewart, who broke in during the heyday of macho superstars like Clark Gable and Errol Flynn, Hanks broke in when glamorous contemporaries like Mel Gibson and Kevin Costner set the bar for leading men. Hanks has made a career of playing ordinary heroes with uncommon subtlety and emotional honesty, uncharacteristic of most other leading men of his time.

Born July 9, 1956, in Concord, California, he lived with his father following his parents' divorce. A professional chef, his father constantly uprooted Hanks and his older brother and sister in search of better work. While the life of an itinerant chef didn't offer much in the way of domestic stability, it did fuel Hanks's interest in acting. Left alone for long stretches of time, he would stave off boredom by performing skits for his older siblings.

Even though he was rather shy, Hanks ultimately gravitated toward the stage. In his senior year of high school, his portrayal of Luther Billis in the musical *South Pacific* brought him the first of many acting awards. While attending college for a short time, Hanks worked as a hotel bellman before taking a friend's advice to join the Great Lakes Shakespeare Festival in Ohio as a company intern.

Interning at the festival turned out to be a valuable experience. After three summers, Hanks earned his Actor's Equity card and an unusual career boost from the festival's admiring directors: they fired him so he could collect unemployment while looking for acting work in New York. Scraping by on unemployment insurance, Hanks worked tirelessly to find stage work in off- and off-off-Broadway productions. His persistence earned him a role in an off-Broadway production of Machiavelli's *The Mandrake* and a tip on a movie role.

In 1980, Hanks learned that manager Simon Maslow was looking for an actor to play a small part in a slasher film. Filming for the part lasted only three days — but it paid $800. When Hanks met with Maslow and several agents, he auditioned for the role and subsequently made his film debut in the low-budget horror movie, *He Knows You're Alone* (1980).

Produced by MGM to cash in on the lucrative slasher film craze of the late seventies, *He Knows You're Alone* featured an unstoppable killer who targets brides and bridesmaids. Billed eighth in the cast credits, Hanks plays Elliott, a psychology student who escorts a couple of girls to a carnival. Although the film had the requisite multiple murders and a *Psycho*-inspired shower scene, Hanks's character survived the carnage. Despite the popularity of B-movie slasher films, the film quickly disappeared from theaters.

With limited prospects on the horizon, Hanks tried his luck at television auditions, and snared one of the lead roles in the pilot for the ABC sitcom *Bosom Buddies,* which the network ultimately picked up for the fall season. An homage to *Some Like It Hot* (1959), *Bosom Buddies* pairs Hanks with Peter Scolari as two advertising copywriters who dress up as women to share a cheap apartment in a women-only residence. What could have

been another mindless, slapdash comedy surprised many with its energy and sharp repartee. This was due in no small part to Hanks and Scolari, who reportedly labored over every script to raise it above the level of the normal sitcom. Their efforts weren't enough to boost the Nielsen ratings, however, and ABC canceled the show after only two seasons.

Guest spots on various sitcoms and television movies paid the bills until Hanks won the lead in Ron Howard's mermaid comedy *Splash* (1984), in which he plays opposite Daryl Hannah. A surprise hit, *Splash* set Hanks on a sure course to movie stardom.

**Hanks portrays
ordinary heroes
with uncommon subtlety
and emotional honesty.**

AL PACINO

Movies provided an early and satisfying outlet for young Pacino, whose restless creativity often manifested itself in youthful troublemaking. Born in East Harlem, New York, on April 25, 1940, Pacino spent most of his childhood with his grandparents in the Bronx after his parents divorced. Family outings were infrequent for the little boy, except for occasional trips to the local movie theater with his mother. Pacino would later reenact much of what he saw for his appreciative grandparents. Since he was uninspired by schoolwork, Pacino's teachers encouraged him to pursue acting.

His mother's illness temporarily derailed Pacino's dreams of becoming a professional actor. He dropped out of high school at sixteen to help his grandfather support the family. Employment options were limited for the high school dropout, who ended up working as a restroom attendant and building superintendent. Despite the humbling nature of this work, Pacino retained dreams of stardom and vowed to return to acting once he'd saved enough money.

Off-Broadway shows established Pacino as a talent to watch. His performance in the 1966 drama *Why is a Crooked Letter* brought him an Obie nomination; he lost to Dustin Hoffman, to whom he was constantly compared in those early days. The next year he played a terrorizing drug-crazed hood in the play, *The Indian Wants the Bronx,* and won an Obie for his performance. Pacino was also accepted as a member of the coveted Actor's Studio, where he was befriended by acting coach Lee Strasberg.

Pacino, after making a name for himself on the Broadway stage, carefully chose his first leading role in a film as Bobby in The Panic in Needle Park (1971).

The year 1969 was a busy one for Pacino. He made his first Broadway stage appearance in *Does the Tiger Wear a Necktie?* The play closed after only 39 performances, but he was praised for his magnificent work as a psychotic junkie, and subsequently won his first Tony Award for Best Actor. That same year Pacino made his film debut with a bit part in *Me, Natalie,* starring Patty Duke. It took only one day to shoot his scene, in which he introduces himself to a potential dance partner, but Pacino later said he felt as though he had covered miles of dance floor in the process.

With the help of an agent, the young actor reviewed and turned down several movie offers before settling on *The Panic in Needle Park* (1971), a love story set among the heroin addicts of New York's Sherman Square. Pacino plays a drug dealer and junkie who leads his girlfriend down the same path. He and co-star Kitty Winn researched the role by visiting treatment centers and areas known for drug peddling.

A year after his first leading role, Pacino's real breakout role came as Michael Corleone in The Godfather (1972).

The movie was not a favorite of moviegoers, probably due to its dark and depressing theme. One critic called it "almost physically painful to watch." The actors were praised for their work, however. Esquire critic Jacob Brinkman wrote, "The entire cast, especially Al Pacino and Kitty Winn in the leads, create intensely real people. Their brand of realness feels close to documentary."

It was this performance that convinced Francis Ford Coppola and Mario Puzo to hire Pacino for the pivotal role of Michael Corleone in *The Godfather,* though the competition he faced was impressive — Jack Nicholson, Warren Beatty, and Robert Redford. Released in 1972, the movie earned Pacino his first Oscar nomination, for Best Supporting Actor. He followed *The Godfather* with a string of classic films, including *Serpico* (1973) and *The Godfather Part II* (1974), which brought him Oscar nominations and confirmed his status as a major movie star.

Since he was uninspired by schoolwork, Pacino's teachers encouraged him to pursue acting.

BRAD PITT

Before starring in films, Pitt was primarily a TV actor in roles such as Billy Canton in the television film Too Young to Die (1989).

His first gig in Hollywood was as a greeter at the El Pollo Loco fast food restaurant, where he wore a feathered chicken costume.

Pitt, as J.D., seducing co-star Geena Davis in Thelma & Louise (1991), the role that solidified Pitt's status as one of Hollywood's up-and-coming leading men.

In the years since he shot to stardom with a scene-stealing turn in *Thelma & Louise* (1991), Pitt has tried to downplay his Hollywood hunk status by taking idiosyncratic roles rather than acting in standard Hollywood star vehicles. While both audience and critical reaction to these films has been decidedly mixed, Pitt has accepted the disappointments with the same easygoing charm, likability, and relaxed self-assurance that have made him a star.

The oldest of three children, Pitt was born in Shawnee, Oklahoma, in 1963, and grew up in Springfield, Missouri, "The Queen City of the Ozarks." A Southern Baptist choirboy and solid student, Pitt enrolled in the University of Missouri to study journalism. In 1985, less than two weeks and two credits short of graduating, he dropped out to head west and test his prospects as a Hollywood actor.

What Pitt found, however, was a series of menial, low-paying jobs that barely paid the rent. At one point, he stood outside the El Pollo Loco fast food restaurant at the intersection of Sunset Boulevard and La Brea Avenue, greeting customers in a yellow, feathered chicken costume. Mann's Chinese Theater and the Hollywood Walk of Fame were within walking distance, but they might as well have been halfway around the world to the struggling actor.

An evening job chauffeuring strippers for a strip-o-gram company provided Pitt with an unlikely entrée into legitimate acting jobs. Many of the strippers were aspiring actresses. One referred him to her acting coach, Roy London. London saw the raw potential in the polite Midwesterner and accepted him into his classes. Then, in an "only in Hollywood" scenario, a young actress asked Pitt to read with her at an audition for an agent. The agent passed on the girl, but signed Pitt as a client.

With his looks and muscular physique, the blonde-haired, blue-eyed Pitt soon found steady, if unspectacular, work on television. Stints on *Dallas* and sitcoms like *Growing Pains* kept him employed, albeit typecast as the high school hunk. He also worked as an extra in the feature *Less Than Zero* (1987), starring Robert Downey Jr. and Andrew McCarthy. What Pitt was looking for was a breakout role, a part in a major film that would propel him to the front ranks. His first film role as a high school hunk in the schlocky horror comedy *Cutting Class* (1989) was hardly the fulfillment of his ambitions.

Co-starring with Roddy McDowall and Martin Mull, Pitt portrays Dwight, the bumbling hunk who chases a killer in this send-up of slasher horror films. A disaster on all fronts, *Cutting Class* did nothing to further Pitt's big-screen aspirations. Down but not out, he returned to television, where he starred in the short-lived series *Glory Days* and the TV movie *Too Young to Die?* (1990), which paired him with future girlfriend Juliette Lewis.

The following year, Pitt finally got the big-screen break that had previously eluded him. When William Baldwin passed on *Thelma and Louise* to star in *Backdraft*, Pitt stepped in to play J.D., the polite, larcenous hitchhiker who seduces the runaway housewife played by Geena Davis and steals all her money. A small but showy role, J.D. gave Pitt the chance to show off his swaggering, southern charm. A pop culture phenomenon, *Thelma and Louise* hit a nerve with audiences, particularly women. Davis and co-star Susan Sarandon may have reaped most of the publicity, but the film nonetheless marked a turning point in Pitt's career. No longer consigned to playing the high school hunk, Pitt began landing substantial roles in major motion pictures.

JULIA ROBERTS

This girl next door's screen persona is an intriguing mix of contradictions. A willowy and poised beauty, Julia Roberts has a raucous, full-bodied laugh and a giddy comic sensibility. Her best performances have an energy and wit that endear her to audiences, who respond to her easy smile and natural warmth. Yet what truly makes Roberts special is a unique girlish sex appeal that is enhanced by the obvious intelligence she brings to her characters.

The youngest in a family of amateur actors, Julie Fiona Roberts was born on October 28, 1967 in Atlanta, and spent most of her childhood in the nearby small town of Smyrna, Georgia. The family home was the frequent site of workshops her parents conducted for local actors and playwrights. Before she was ten, Roberts had to endure both her parents' divorce and her father's subsequent death. The loss of her father was devastating to the shy little girl, who had been close to both parents.

Although she had participated in her parents' workshops, Roberts originally viewed acting as no more than a lark — not a viable career choice. While her older siblings pursued acting careers in New York, Roberts wavered between studying journalism and veterinary science. Yet when she graduated from high school in 1985, Roberts abandoned those plans to focus on acting. She left Smyrna to join siblings Eric and Lisa in New York.

By this time, her older brother Eric had established a film career with acclaimed performances in *King of the Gypsies* (1979) and *Star 80* (1983). Julia Roberts's acting experience then consisted of a few plays and the family's workshops — hardly a noteworthy or promising resume, especially in the highly competitive and crowded New York acting world. A thick Southern accent was a further handicap for the aspiring actress. To make ends meet, she worked at Baskin-Robbins and later modeled for the Click Agency between acting classes.

Despite her inexperience, Roberts did have an undeniable spark that set her apart from other hopefuls, and it was immediately recognized by talent agent Mary Sames. Rather than sign Roberts, however, Sames referred her to personal manager Bob McGowan, who had a reputation for nurturing young talent. He promptly sent Roberts to acting classes and a speech coach to get rid of her Georgia drawl.

Within a year of earning her high school diploma, Roberts landed her first movie: *Blood Red* (1986), starring her brother Eric, Giancarlo Giannini, and Dennis Hopper. At her brother's suggestion, she was hired at the last minute for the small role of his younger sister in this family drama set in late nineteenth century California. Playing Maria, the daughter of a Sicilian winegrower (Giannini), Roberts only has a few lines and even less chance to project the magnetic personality that would later make her a star. She is a peripheral character in the story, which pits railroad baron Hopper against Giannini in a battle for land. Hardly a star vehicle, *Blood Red* at least gave Roberts much-needed experience and professional legitimacy.

Due to financial difficulties, *Blood Red*'s release was delayed until 1988. Roberts's second film, *Satisfaction,* therefore made it into movie theaters first. A low-budget teen comedy about an all-girl rock and roll band, *Satisfaction* is primarily a vehicle for television actress Justine Bateman, who plays the group's lead singer. Roberts takes a supporting role as bass player Darryle Shane, a sexy free spirit who spends most of the time in her boyfriend's van. The film certainly gives Roberts more screen time than *Blood Red,* but it is forgettable fare that quickly disappeared in the wake of negative reviews and lackluster box office sales. It was not until Roberts landed the role of Daisy, a fun-loving, pizza parlor waitress in the ensemble sleeper *Mystic Pizza* (1988), that Roberts's screen career finally hit full stride. Within a few years she became the highest-paid actress in film history.

> ## "I've sort of grown into my cuteness."
>
> — Julia Roberts,
> reflecting on her awkward
> adolescence

Movie audiences first saw Roberts in Satisfaction (1988), a low budget teen comedy. Also pictured: Justine Bateman (left).

Mystic Pizza (1988), released months after her film debut, offered Roberts (far right) a chance to break out as an up-and-coming star. Also pictured: Annabeth Gish (left) and Lili Taylor.

MEG RYAN

Ryan (opposite Candice Bergen) in her feature-film debut, as Debby, in Rich and Famous (1981).

Ryan was a standout in high school, where she was elected homecoming queen.

Ryan eating at Katz's Delicatessen with co-star Billy Crystal, in When Harry Met Sally (1989), in a scene that made her famous.

With her warm smile, perky personality and blonde hair, Meg Ryan invites comparisons to thirties star Jean Arthur; like Arthur, Ryan projects a down-to-earth, no-nonsense intelligence in every role. To avoid being typecast as the girl next door, Ryan consistently seeks out challenging material. She has convincingly played roles as diverse as an alcoholic mother, a decorated Gulf War soldier, and an exotic dancer. It is in the arena of romantic comedy, however, that Ryan has become a star.

The daughter of a high school math teacher and aspiring actress, Margaret Mary Emily Anne Hyra was born November 19, 1961, in Fairfield, Connecticut. When Ryan was fifteen, her mother left the family to pursue an acting career. In spite of the upheaval at home, Ryan was a standout in high school, where she was elected homecoming queen.

Ryan went on to college, declaring a major in journalism. "My first goal was to be a writer," she once told *Daytime TV* magazine. "What I really wanted … was to be a reporter and travel." While in school, she appeared in commercials to earn money for college. She obtained a Screen Actors Guild card using her mother's maiden name of Ryan in 1980. Whether she had planned it or not, Meg Ryan had become an actress.

After two years of college, she won the role of Debby in director George Cukor's final movie, *Rich and Famous,* in 1981. A remake of the 1943 Bette Davis film *Old Acquaintance, Rich and Famous* stars Candice Bergen and Jacqueline Bisset as two lifelong friends who become successful authors and bitter rivals. Ryan plays Bergen's 18-year-old daughter, who dumps her own boyfriend in favor of Bisset's.

Although her part is small, Ryan makes the most of her screen time, holding her own opposite both Bergen and Bisset. Afterward, she admitted that she was overwhelmed by the entire experience; she had never even been on an airplane, and suddenly she was on a movie set being directed by one of Hollywood's most acclaimed directors. A glossy melodrama, *Rich and Famous* opened to mixed reviews and only fair box office.

Encouraged by her success, Ryan dropped out of college to devote her time to becoming an actress. She landed a role in the ABC Afterschool Special *Amy and the Angel.* A steady paycheck came with a regular role on the CBS soap opera *As the World Turns,* in 1982, as Betsy Stewart Montgomery Andropolous, who endures the standard mix of marital discord and bizarre plot twists that characterize soap operas. A fan favorite, Ryan played the role for two years before leaving the series to return to the big screen. Supporting roles came her way, but nothing that really gave Ryan a chance to stand out from the thousands of young actresses in Hollywood. A small but pivotal role in 1986's *Top Gun* finally gave Ryan the chance to shine. As a fighter pilot's wife, Ryan demonstrates both her comedic flair and dramatic abilities. Three years later, Ryan finally became a star in Rob Reiner's *When Harry Met Sally* (1989).

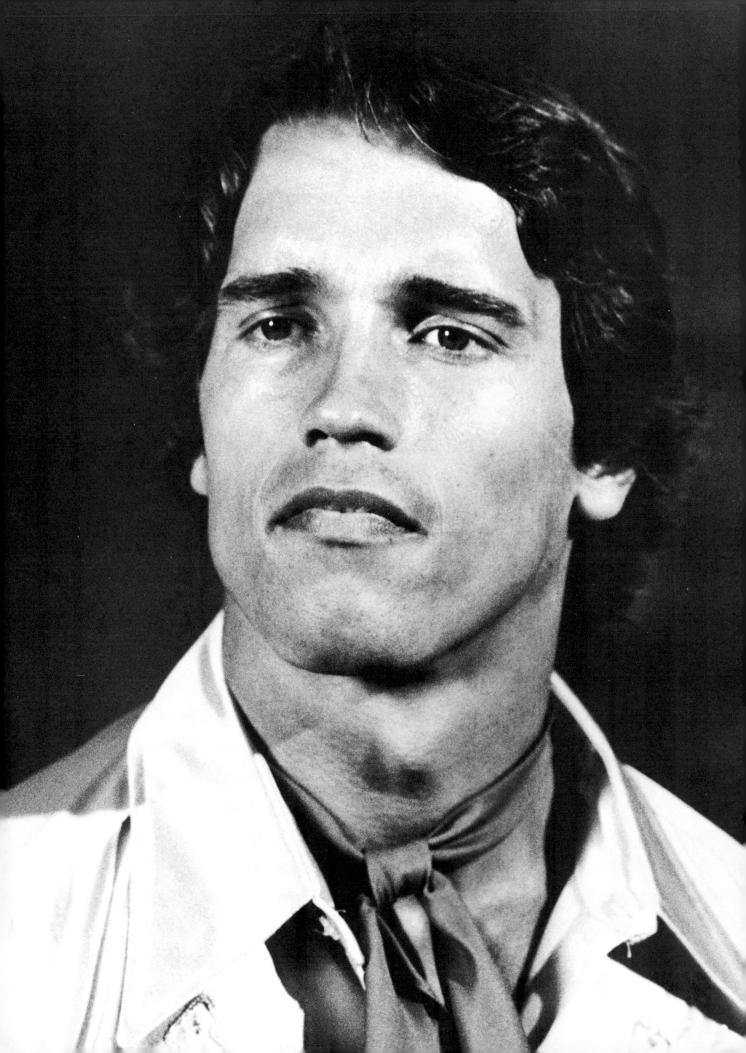

ARNOLD SCHWARZENEGGER

Arnold Schwarzenegger has dodged the pitfalls that trapped Steve Reeves and other muscle-bound screen heroes. Often underestimated, he made it to stardom by shrewdly emphasizing his strengths and downplaying his weaknesses — namely, his thick Austrian accent and bodybuilder's presence, which could have easily relegated him to playing the muscular goon in straight-to-video fare. Not only did Schwarzenegger work to minimize his accent, but he also selected projects where dialogue was secondary to action. Although he has a surprising comic flair, Schwarzenegger truly became a star when the market for action films exploded in the eighties.

The bodybuilder-turned-actor who once billed himself as "The Austrian Oak" was born on July 30, 1947, in the rural town of Graz, Austria. His father hoped he would become a professional soccer player, but Schwarzenegger preferred weight lifting and diligently built and toned his physique to win several European contests, including Mr. Olympia. A driven and pragmatic youth, he left Austria for the United States, where he studied both business and economics at the University of Wisconsin and competed in bodybuilding exhibitions. Keenly aware that bodybuilding alone would never make him rich, Schwarzenegger invested his prize winnings in real estate and started a mail-order bodybuilding equipment company that made him a millionaire before his twenty-second birthday.

Having gone as far as he could as a bodybuilder, Schwarzenegger decided to try his hand at acting. In 1970 he made his film debut credited as "Arnold Strong" in the low-budget spoof *Hercules in New York;* not only did the film's producers consider his real last name too unwieldy for the marquee, but they also dubbed his voice, thereby reducing Schwarzenegger's role to little more than a moving mannequin. Cast as the Olympian hero sent to contemporary New York by accident, his character wreaks havoc in Manhattan, until he falls for a college professor's pretty daughter, who tutors him in the ways of the city. Their romance ends when Zeus sends his minions to bring his wayward son back to Mount Olympus.

The reception given *Hercules in New York* did not bode well for Schwarzenegger's film career. Embarrassed, he retreated to the gym and also began taking acting lessons in earnest. Aside from a cameo role as a hood in *The Long Goodbye* (1973), Schwarzenegger steered clear of the big screen until director Bob Rafelson approached him with a role specifically tailored to his talents: Austrian bodybuilder Joe Santo in the comedy-drama *Stay Hungry* (1976).

Based on the novel by Charles Gaines, *Stay Hungry* depicts the friendship that develops between a rich Southern playboy (Jeff Bridges) and Santo, who works in a Birmingham, Alabama gym and plays bluegrass fiddle in his spare time. Speaking in his own voice, Schwarzenegger gives a natural, relaxed performance that surprised audiences and critics alike, who had previously written him off as just another slab of beefcake. Presented at the 1976 Venice Film Festival, *Stay Hungry* was too offbeat for mainstream audiences and did only moderate business at the box office. For Schwarzenegger, however, *Stay Hungry* was enough to keep him in Hollywood. Six years would pass before he landed a role equally suited to . his talents — the title role in *Conan the Barbarian* (1982).

Schwarzenegger (credited as "Arnold Strong") in his feature-film debut — Hercules in New York (1970.

His father hoped he would become a professional soccer player, but Schwarzenegger preferred weight lifting.

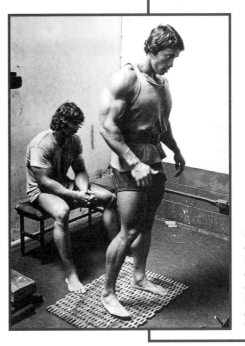

Schwarzenegger achieved international celebrity when he appeared as himself in the 1977 documentary Pumping Iron.

SYLVESTER STALLONE

Stallone (second from left) in The Lords of Flatbush (1974) — his first leading role. Also pictured: Perry King (far left), Paul Mace (back to camera), and Henry Winkler, also in his first film.

"That's what Rocky's all about: pride, reputation, and not being another bum in the neighborhood."

— Stallone
on his star-making performance

The role for which Stallone will always be remembered — Rocky Balboa in the Oscar-winning film Rocky (1976).

Success in Hollywood did not come easily for "Sly" Stallone. His career is all the more remarkable in light of his traumatic childhood in New York's rough Hell's Kitchen. His troubles literally began in the delivery room on July 6, 1946, when the doctor's forceps slipped and severed the infant's facial nerve, resulting in partial paralysis of his lip, tongue, and chin. Mercilessly teased for his permanently droopy lower lip, crooked left eye, and slurred speech, Stallone found little relief at home, where his parents bickered incessantly. Their fighting escalated to the point that Stallone was in and out of foster homes until the family left New York for Silver Spring, Maryland, in the early fifties.

By the time he reached high school, Stallone had been expelled from several schools for violent behavior. His parents had divorced, and at the age of fifteen, Stallone moved with his mother and stepfather to Philadelphia, where he attended a special school for emotionally disturbed youths. Though he continued to receive abysmal grades, Stallone excelled in athletics, especially football, which earned him a scholarship to the American College in Switzerland. There he rediscovered a childhood penchant for acting, earning sustained applause for his performance as Willy Loman in a school production of *Death of a Salesman*.

Upon his return to the United States, Stallone entered the drama school at the University of Miami, where his acting and screenwriting ambitions received little encouragement. He returned to New York before completing his degree, determined to prove himself as an actor. On the basis of his athletic physique, Stallone was frequently advised to seek work in B-movies and soft-core pornography. It was on one such casting call that he earned his first film role in the skin flick, *A Party at Kitty and Stud's* (1970).

As Stud, Stallone parades around a nondescript set, naked except for a pocket watch and a gold pendant necklace. The disjointed plot follows Stud and his girlfriend Kitty through a surreal orgiastic party at their apartment. Much of the screen time is taken up by gratuitous sex scenes not involving Stallone, who never actually engages in sex on camera. He does, however, commit such memorable acts of bad taste as posing in front of a mirror while eyeing a lesbian sex scene in the reflection. Later, Stallone entertains disjointed fantasies of a mystery woman naked in a New York park, before leading a strange hallucinogenic group dance that concludes the movie.

Even by the standards of low-budget, soft-core pornography, *A Party at Kitty and Stud's* is forgettable, an embarrassing blip in Stallone's career. Meanwhile, Stallone's muscular build and menacing features continued to earn him small parts, including a nonspeaking turn as a subway thug in Woody Allen's *Bananas* (1971). Finally, encouraged by his mother's amateur astrological predictions, Stallone decided to test his fate in Hollywood. Aside from a decent role as a fifties-era hood in the ensemble comedy *The Lords of Flatbush* (1974), his career remained stalled, limited to parts in movies like Roger Corman's cult classic *Death Race 2000* (1975). He pinned most of his hopes on screenwriting, but felt little inspiration until watching unknown boxer Chuck Wepner go fifteen rounds with Muhammad Ali. Within a few days, he had completed the screenplay for *Rocky*, a low-budget film that would eventually gross over $200 million, spawn four sequels, and win the 1976 Oscar for Best Picture.

MERYL STREEP

Arguably the finest actress of her generation, Meryl Streep has played an astonishing array of roles since her 1977 debut in *Julia*. Immersing herself both emotionally and physically in her roles, Streep creates utterly different characters in each film. A two-time Oscar winner, she has been nominated for the coveted prize twelve times – a record she shares with Katharine Hepburn.

The silver screen's foremost practitioner of foreign accents hails from Summit, New Jersey, where she was born on June 22, 1949. Streep grew up in the quiet, neighboring town of Basking Ridge, where she developed an early interest in performing. Opera was Streep's first love; she took voice lessons from Beverly Sills's operatic coach while still in junior high. A self-described ugly duckling in glasses, Streep transformed herself with contact lenses and hair dye the summer before high school. The newly glamorous teenager discovered acting in high school, where she starred in several student-sponsored productions between stints as a cheerleader and homecoming queen.

An excellent student, Streep enrolled at Vassar in 1967, and began to study drama in earnest. Her professors were impressed enough to recommend that Streep apply to the prestigious Yale School of Drama. Accepted into the program, she immersed herself in her studies. Even in a setting where every student was extremely talented, Streep stood out. Her reputation carried her to Broadway, where she eventually won a Tony nomination for the musical *Happy End*. Hollywood soon came calling.

Hoping to get Streep under contract to 20th Century Fox, producer Julien Derode suggested her name to veteran director Fred Zinnemann. At the time, Zinnemann was just beginning work on a film adaptation of Lillian Hellman's memoir *Pentimento*. The film, to be titled *Julia,* would recount the friendship between playwright Hellman and her childhood friend Julia, a former debutante turned freedom fighter in Nazi Germany. Initially, Zinnemann envisioned a little-known but accomplished actress in the title role, so Streep seemed to fit the bill. To explore the matter further, Zinnemann invited her to meet with him in England, where Streep's poise and charisma immediately impressed him. He toyed with casting her for the part of Julia until studio executives pushed for the more established Vanessa Redgrave.

With Jane Fonda slated to play the role of Lillian, Zinnemann had to call Streep with a disappointing offer: the smaller part of Anne Marie, an old high school acquaintance of Lillian's. She agreed to take the part, though with some understandable hesitation. Anne Marie is detestable — unctuously phony, persistently selfish and even involved in an incestuous relationship with her brother. Despite her initial reservations, Streep played the part with utmost skill, making Anne Marie the sort of character viewers love to hate.

Her next role, in Michael Cimino's Vietnam epic *The Deer Hunter,* was more sympathetic. Playing a sensitive young woman abused by her father and trapped by economic circumstances in a Pennsylvania steel town, Streep received her first Oscar nomination for Best Supporting Actress. Over the next fifteen years, she would become a familiar face at the Academy Awards.

> **"Meryl embodies everything a great, worthwhile artist is about."**
>
> — James Woods

Streep (opposite Robert De Niro) was nominated for an Oscar for The Deer Hunter *(1978), her first leading role.*

Streep in the wedding party sequence in The Deer Hunter.

JOHN TRAVOLTA

> **Both parents supported the children's acting ambitions; Travolta's father even built a wooden stage in the family's basement so the children could perform for neighbors.**

Though hardly by his own design, John Travolta's journey to stardom is neatly divided into two chapters. In the late seventies, his status as a teen heartthrob and television star evolved into genuine film stardom with the phenomenal success of *Saturday Night Fever* (1977) and *Grease* (1978). Then his star descended, and his career appeared to be almost over. Things would change in the nineties.

The youngest of six children, Travolta was born on February 18, 1954, in Englewood, New Jersey, to devout Catholics who pronounced his unexpected arrival a miracle. Doted on from birth, Travolta grew up in a loving household where his mother encouraged the children to express themselves creatively. Both parents supported the children's acting ambitions; Travolta's father even built a wooden stage in the family's basement so the children could perform for the neighbors.

His heart set on becoming an actor, Travolta moved beyond the basement stage to enroll in a local drama workshop and study tap dancing with Gene Kelly's younger brother. With his parents' blessing, Travolta left high school at the age of sixteen to pursue acting full-time. He began by performing in local musicals and dinner-theater productions, but in an open casting call he landed a small part in the 1972 off-Broadway play *Rain*. The next year Travolta joined a touring production of *Grease,* playing the bit part of Doody, which he followed with his first Broadway role in *Over Here!* starring the Andrews Sisters.

Travolta's breakthrough year was 1975. His agent encouraged him to move to Hollywood, where an open casting call led to his film debut in *The Devil's Rain.* A cheap supernatural thriller shot on location in Mexico, *The Devil's Rain* is not exactly an actor's showcase. Travolta plays Danny, a local teenager who is turned into a zombie by a group of Satanists led by Ernest Borgnine. In heavy make-up, a barely recognizable Travolta speaks one line before he and the other zombies melt into a gooey mess at the film's climax: "Blasphemer! Get him, he is a blasphemer!" A laughably bad attempt to cash in on *The Exorcist* (1973), *The Devil's Rain* represents a low point for veteran actors Ernest Borgnine, Ida Lupino, and Eddie Albert, among others. The film disappeared without a trace, only to resurface in 1977 as producers tried to capitalize on Travolta's stardom.

After the debacle of *The Devil's Rain,* Travolta auditioned for a television series called *Welcome Back, Kotter.* Handpicked by series creator and star Gabe Kaplan for the role of Vinnie Barbarino, a dim but good-natured high school hunk, Travolta quickly became a teen idol. It was a mixed blessing for Travolta, who wanted to be taken seriously as an actor, not as a *Tiger Beat* cover model. Eager to prove his range, he signed on to play the title role in the 1976 made-for-TV movie *The Boy in the Plastic Bubble.*

Travolta's big break came in 1975, when he was cast as Vinnie Barbarino (right) in the hit TV sitcom Welcome Back, Kotter.

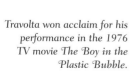

Travolta won acclaim for his performance in the 1976 TV movie The Boy in the Plastic Bubble.

A poignant coming-of-age drama about a young man who has spent his entire life inside a plastic bubble because of a weakened immune system, *The Boy in the Plastic Bubble* is a fine showcase for Travolta. As Tod Lubitsch, he gives a sensitive, understated performance that vividly captures the unusual plight of a boy aching for physical contact. There is no trace of Vinnie Barbarino's swagger or mannerisms in Travolta's performance, much to the welcome surprise of many critics. A ratings smash, *The Boy in the Plastic Bubble* served notice that Travolta had the makings of a major star. *Saturday Night Fever* and an Oscar nomination followed a year later.

Travolta continued his meteoric ascent when he scored box office success as Tony Manero in the 1977 film Saturday Night Fever.

DENZEL WASHINGTON

A magnetic, versatile actor, Denzel Washington is never less than convincing, even when the material doesn't seem to fit his persona. As director Kenneth Branagh once remarked, "Denzel Washington has intellectual weight, spiritual gravity, and a powerful sexual and romantic presence."

Born on December 28, 1954, in Mount Vernon, New York, to a Pentecostal preacher and a beautician, Washington was raised with a strong work ethic, a passion for performance and an appreciation for the art of storytelling. When he was twelve he began working at a local barbershop, where he listened attentively to the stories around him. His parents divorced when he was fourteen, and Washington finished his early education at a boarding school. He went on to college at Fordham University, intending to study journalism, but a summer job with the YMCA gave him a taste of acting, and he returned to his fall classes with a new focus. Upon graduation, Washington was accepted at the prestigious American Conservatory Theater (ACT) in San Francisco.

Unlike many actors who bide their time with odd jobs or waiting tables, Washington was lucky enough to land his first acting job even before he graduated from Fordham. A professor convinced several agents to see Washington in a school production of *Othello*. His impressive performance in the title role led to Washington's debut in the 1977 made-for-TV movie *Wilma*.

The movie depicts the life of African-American track star Wilma Rudolph, who in 1960 overcame physical handicaps to win three Olympic medals. Washington is the film's male lead, Rudolph's boyfriend Robert Eldridge. Washington later said that he experienced a healthy dose of fear the first day on the set. Viewers merely saw a younger version of the poised and confident actor audiences know today.

After filming, Washington headed for San Francisco and the ACT. After a year with the school, he left for New York, where he was given the chance to play Malcolm X, a role he would play again in 1992 to unanimous critical acclaim, in the off-Broadway production of *When the Chickens Come Home to Roost*. This was his first chance to research a part thoroughly. Washington read articles, listened to speeches and watch taped footage to make his portrayal of the slain leader as authentic as possible. The play's run was short — just twelve performances — but the work was rewarding. Washington received critical acclaim for his performance and the interest of producer/screenwriter Stanley Shapiro, who was looking for a young African-American actor to star in the comedy *Carbon Copy* (1981). Shapiro had been meeting with dozens of actors for the role of Roger Porter, the 17-year-old illegitimate son of a white corporate executive (George Segal), but none seemed equipped to handle the role's serio-comic demands. Washington's tour-de-force stage performance convinced the veteran producer that he could bring Porter to life and hold his own against Segal onscreen.

A labored, predictable comedy, *Carbon Copy* is not one of Shapiro's most inspired efforts. The sharp wit that brought Shapiro an Oscar for *Pillow Talk* (1959) is conspicuously absent from *Carbon Copy*, which rarely rises above the level of an average sitcom. Washington is still impressive in a thankless role, while Segal overacts as the executive brought crashing down to earth by his son's arrival. When big-screen stardom failed to materialize as a result of *Carbon Copy*, Washington returned to television and a recurring role on the medical drama *St. Elsewhere*. After a six-year run, Washington left the Emmy-winning series, soon to become an Academy Award-winning movie star.

> ## "Washington has intellectual weight, spiritual gravity and a powerful sexual and romantic presence."
>
> — Kenneth Branagh

Washington with co-star George Segal in Carbon Copy (1981), Washington's first film.

Washington helps co-star Segal after a hard day's work shoveling horse manure in Carbon Copy.

ROBIN WILLIAMS

Williams landed his own TV sitcom — Mork and Mindy (above) — after a successful TV appearance on the hit show, Happy Days.

Williams, as the title character in Popeye (1980), his first leading movie role.

From the beginning of his acting career in the seventies, Williams's sensitivity, combined with his take-no-prisoners brand of comedy, has earned him increasingly complex roles in Hollywood. He reportedly owes his big break to director Garry Marshall's son, who was seven years old at the time. When Marshall was overseeing the popular sitcom *Happy Days* in the late seventies, his son came up with the idea of having an alien visit the Cunningham family. One of the twenty comedians selected to audition for the role of Mork, Williams landed the role when Marshall asked him to sit down during his audition; the comedian went to the nearest chair and promptly sat on his head. As Marshall later explained, "He was the only alien who auditioned."

Since that big break, the whirling dervish stand-up comedian has been free-associating and improvising comic riffs that often spiral off into the absurd, yet somehow ring of truth. With his rubbery, court jester features and boundless energy, Williams enlivens even the most pedestrian screen comedies.

Humor has long been a coping mechanism for Williams, who was born July 21, 1952, in Chicago, to a Ford Motor executive and former model. A pudgy, bookish child, Williams spent his childhood in Detroit and his adolescence in affluent Marin County, California. By the time he reached high school, he had slimmed down and found his niche as the class clown.

Williams entered college as a political science major, but later switched to theater arts after joining an improvisation group. He graduated from Marin Junior College and applied to the prestigious Juilliard School in New York. For most aspiring actors, Juilliard would be the equivalent of theatrical nirvana. Although Williams studied for two years under John Houseman, he felt confined by the curriculum and left to pursue stand-up, first in San Francisco and then at The Comedy Store in Los Angeles, where he landed a residency worth $200 a week.

Veteran television producer George Schlatter caught Williams's act at The Comedy Store and approached him about appearing in a revival of the 1960s *Laugh-In* show. For $1,500 a week, Williams found it hard to refuse and signed on for the series, which lasted only fourteen weeks. A critical bomb, *Laugh-In* nonetheless led to Williams joining the cast of the highly touted *Richard Pryor Show*, which NBC unadvisedly scheduled during the family hour. A network censor's nightmare from the first episode, the series was also canceled after a short run.

Turning from television to the big screen, Williams made his film debut in a low-budget sex comedy entitled *Can I Do It ... Till I Need Glasses?* (1977), which was little more than a loose collection of raunchy skits. Although Williams appears only briefly in the film, *Can I Do It ... Till I Need Glasses?* subsequently came back to haunt him when the producers re-released it to cash in on Williams's newfound celebrity during the heyday of the sitcom *Mork and Mindy.*

Williams's luck had changed following his guest appearance as Mork from Ork on *Happy Days*. In 1978, ABC created a spin-off series, *Mork and Mindy*, which gave Williams ample opportunity to ad-lib with co-star Pam Dawber, who plays an ordinary

woman faced with the challenge of sheltering Williams's alien character. What could have been a one-joke premise turned into a showcase for Williams's hilarious improvisations. It was then unheard of for a cast member to depart from the three jokes per page sitcom standard, but once they adjusted to Williams's comic sensibility, the series's writers left blank pages in the scripts to accommodate the star.

Impressed by his TV success, Paramount and Disney offered Williams the title role in their new film, *Popeye,* in 1980. Based on the cartoon character, the movie focuses on Popeye's search for his father and his attempt to win the heart of Olive Oyl. In spite of Williams's talent, the film was a dismal failure, panned by the public and critics alike.

Although he appeared in several more films, Williams didn't make his mark in movies until 1987 with his performance in *Good Morning, Vietnam.* The role of Adrian Cronauer, an irreverent American disc jockey, allowed him to do what he did best — improvise. The film was a success, earning him his first Academy Award nomination.

"He was the only alien who auditioned."

— Producer Garry Marshall about casting Williams's alien role in *Mork and Mindy.*

THE BRAT PACK

In the late seventies and early eighties, the studios began aggressively courting younger moviegoers. Bittersweet comedies of teen angst and rebellion became a staple at the multiplex, as adolescents forked over their allowances again and again to watch youthful protagonists negotiate the rocky road to adulthood — usually to a soundtrack of hit singles. Dubbed the "Brat Pack," a group of young actors briefly ruled the box office before falling from professional grace, the victims of overexposure and encroaching adulthood.

Emilio Estevez comes from a family of actors, including father Martin Sheen and brother Charlie Sheen. It's no surprise then that his acting career began while he was still a teenager and that his film debut came in the 1982 movie, *Tex,* when he was just twenty years old. He appeared in several other Brat Pack films, including 1985's *St. Elmo's Fire* and *The Breakfast Club.*

Rob Lowe was an experienced actor by the time he joined the Brat Pack. He appeared in over thirty plays in his youth, starting when he was just eight years old. At nineteen he debuted in his first feature film, *The Outsiders* (1983). His other Brat Pack movies include *About Last Night* (1986) and *St. Elmo's Fire.*

Demi Moore, née Demetria Guynes, was a former model before she got her first break as Jackie Templeton in the daytime soap opera, *General Hospital.* She first appeared on the big screen in the 1981 film, *Choices.* Moore's career got a boost, however, when she appeared as the self-destructive party girl in *St. Elmo's Fire.* Moore survived the Brat Pack to become one of the top stars of the nineties, appearing in such blockbusters as *Ghost* (1990) and *Indecent Proposal* (1993).

Judd Nelson's first acting experience was purely accidental. He was watching a friend try out for a play and was told only those auditioning could stay. Taking a chance, he auditioned and got the part. He later studied acting with Stella Adler and landed his first film role starring opposite Kevin Costner in the ensemble drama, *Fandango* (1985). *St. Elmo's Fire* and *The Breakfast Club* are two of the Brat Pack films on his resume.

Molly Ringwald began singing at the age of three and a half, and went on to record her first jazz album at age six. Branching out, she began to act in community theater productions, including *Annie.* She appeared on *The New Mickey Mouse Club* before landing her first movie role in *Tempest* (1982), when she was thirteen. The muse of Brat Pack auteur John Hughes, she starred in *Sixteen Candles* (1984), *The Breakfast Club* and *Pretty in Pink* (1986).

Ally Sheedy is more than just an actress: by age six she was dancing at Lincoln Center with the American Ballet Theater; at twelve she wrote a best-selling children's book, *She Was Nice to Mice.* She turned to acting at fifteen, starting with commercials and moving on to TV guest appearances. Her first film role was as Sean Penn's girlfriend in the 1983 movie, *Bad Boys.* She appeared in two classic Brat Pack films, *St. Elmo's Fire* and *The Breakfast Club.*

(top to bottom) Emilio Estevez, Rob Lowe, Demi Moore, Judd Nelson, Molly Ringwald, Ally Sheedy

STAND-UP STARS

Billy Crystal   Whoopi Goldberg   Steve Martin   Eddie Murphy

Like the vaudeville performers before them, stand-up comedians found the silver screen a perfect medium to display their larger-than-life talents. Many comedians who made the switch from the stage to film or television went on to become some of Hollywood's biggest stars. In fact, some of the greatest comedic actors in recent memory got their start performing in front of small crowds on the comedy club circuit. But as the saying goes, all the world loves a clown.

Billy Crystal's family was in the music business, so it was only natural that the talented young boy would develop a fascination with the performing arts. He started doing comedy routines at a young age, and after attending NYU film school, the stand-up comedian made the transition from the stage to television. In 1978, Crystal made his big-screen debut in the comedy, *Rabbit Test,* a flop about the world's first pregnant man. In 1984, he landed a part on *Saturday Night Live,* which he then parlayed into film stardom with memorable roles in such hits as *When Harry Met Sally* (1989) and *City Slickers* (1991).

Whoopi Goldberg was born Caryn Johnson in New York City. As a child she appeared on Broadway in a variety of small roles. She left New York for California, however, and began performing in comedy troupes up and down the coast. The talented comic had a hit one-woman stage show on Broadway that led to her starring role in Steven Spielberg's adaptation of the Pulitzer Prize-winning novel, *The Color Purple* (1985). Oscar-nominated for her performance, she later won the Oscar for Best Supporting Actress for *Ghost* (1990).

Steve Martin got his start entertaining children at Disneyland. While attending UCLA, Martin realized that entertaining was in his blood, and after earning his degree in theater arts, he found himself writing for the hit TV show, *The Smothers Brothers Comedy Hour.* He started to appear on variety shows himself, but it wasn't until he hit the road with his own comedy act that he became recognized as a legitimate comedian. In 1977, Martin made his film debut in the Oscar-nominated comedy short, *The Absent-Minded Waiter.* After a cameo in *Sgt. Pepper's Lonely Hearts Club Band* (1978), Martin became a genuine movie star in the title role of *The Jerk* (1979).

Eddie Murphy started his stand-up act when he was just fifteen, appearing in local bars and clubs in suburban Long Island, New York. After graduating from high school, Murphy hit the comedy clubs of New York City. He eventually landed a spot on *Saturday Night Live* at the tender age of nineteen. Two years later, in 1982, Murphy made his big-screen debut in the hit action comedy, *48 Hrs.* After that stellar performance, Murphy went on to become one of Hollywood's most popular performers.

OTHER STARS OF THE PERIOD

Jim Carrey   Jodie Foster   Richard Gere   Jessica Lange

Sandra Bullock was a well-traveled child, touring the world with her mother, a German opera singer. After appearing in a number of off-Broadway plays, Bullock eventually made her way to Hollywood, making her film debut in the 1987 thriller, *Hangmen*. After a few more roles in forgettable films, Bullock won the lead in the short-lived sitcom, *Working Girl,* based on the 1988 Melanie Griffith comedy. She persevered, however, and in 1993 she scored a breakthrough by starring opposite Sylvester Stallone in the futuristic thriller, *Demolition Man*. Bullock hit it big in the action smash, *Speed* (1994), which in turn led to the romantic comedy hit, *While You Were Sleeping* (1995).

Jim Carrey, widely regarded as the comic heir apparent to Jerry Lewis, began his career as a stand-up in his native Canada. In 1983 he made his film debut in the low-budget comedy *All in Good Taste,* in which Carrey appears nude except for a strategically placed camera. Eleven years later, he would become a star in *Ace Ventura, Pet Detective* (1994).

George Clooney studied at Northern Kentucky University before he entered the family business. Clooney's father Nick was a successful radio broadcaster, and his aunt Rosemary was a world-famous singer and actress. In 1987, Clooney made his debut in the slasher film, *Return to Horror High*. He later appeared in several television series, ranging from the teen sitcom, *The Facts of Life,* to the primetime drama, *Sisters*. Stardom finally came for Clooney in the early nineties, with a starring role in the hit series, *ER*. He subsequently left *ER* to concentrate on a thriving movie career, with such films as *Batman and Robin* (1997) and the acclaimed *Out of Sight* (1998).

Jodie Foster made her feature film debut at ten in the Walt Disney movie, *Napoleon and Samantha,* in 1972. She later landed several film roles that forced her to play characters well beyond her years, most notably as a teen prostitute in *Taxi Driver* (1976), which brought the precociously talented actress her first Oscar nomination. After dropping out of Hollywood to attend Yale, Foster returned in the late eighties and won Academy Awards for her performances in *The Accused* (1988) and *The Silence of the Lambs* (1991).

Richard Gere, the son of an insurance salesman, was a talented musician who dropped out of the University of Massachusetts to go on the road with several bands. While in Cape Cod, Gere joined the Provincetown Players to hone his acting skills. A few years later, the handsome, mercurial actor landed on Broadway. In 1975, he made his big-screen debut in the police drama *Report to the Commissioner*. His performance as a violent hustler in *Looking for Mr. Goodbar* (1977) boosted Gere's Hollywood profile, but stardom would come with his performance in *American Gigolo* (1980).

Helen Hunt made her debut in the television film *Pioneer Woman* in 1973 and enjoyed much success in that medium, appearing regularly in TV movies, and in the television series *Swiss Family Robinson*. When she was thirteen, she landed her first feature-film role in 1977's *Rollercoaster*. Although she continued wracking up television and film credits, Hunt only became a star after landing a co-starring role in the hit sitcom *Mad About You*. She parlayed her small screen success into big screen stardom and won an Academy Award for 1997's *As Good As It Gets*.

Bette Midler   *Kevin Spacey*   *Oprah Winfrey*

Jessica Lange was born in Cloquet, Minnesota, but her father, a traveling salesman, often moved her around the country. When she was older, she studied at the University of Minnesota before heading to France to study mime and dance. Upon returning to the States, she quickly landed her first movie role in the 1976 remake of *King Kong*, beating out hundreds of aspiring actresses for the part. A big-budget disappointment, the film did little for Lange, who had to wait until 1980 for stardom to come her way with a powerful performance opposite Jack Nicholson in the remake of James M. Cain's *The Postman Always Rings Twice*.

Bette Midler, a talented singer, dancer, and actress, was born in Hawaii in 1945. She studied drama at the University of Hawaii, but left after a year to pursue an acting career. In 1966, she made her big-screen debut as an extra in *Hawaii*, but other roles weren't readily forthcoming, so she headed to New York where she found work as a go-go dancer. She appeared on Broadway and then starred in her own cabaret act as the raunchy and outrageous "Divine Miss M." Her first starring role came in 1979's *The Rose*, in which she plays a hard-living rock singer who bears more than a passing resemblance to Janis Joplin. Midler's tour-de-force performance brought her an Oscar nomination and established her film career.

Michelle Pfeiffer, like many stars before her, won a local beauty contest before embarking on a career as an actress. After the pageant, Pfeiffer started getting work in commercials, which soon led to some minor television gigs (*Fantasy Island* and the short-lived *Delta House*). Her big-screen debut came in 1980's romantic drama *Falling in Love Again*. Her movie career was slow going after that, but after a strong performance as the cocaine-addled trophy wife of a Cuban drug dealer in *Scarface* (1983), Pfeiffer was set for stardom.

Burt Reynolds might have been a professional football player if an auto accident hadn't sidelined his career at Florida State University. He changed his focus to drama and eventually dropped out of school to try his luck on Broadway. It took two years before Universal signed him to a TV contract and used him in such popular shows as *Gunsmoke* and *Dan August*. His first film work was as a stuntman. In 1961 Reynolds made his movie debut appearing in *Angel Baby* and *Armored Command*. It was 1972, however, before he made a name for himself in *Deliverance*. He was one of Hollywood's top box-office draws throughout the 70s and early 80s.

Kevin Spacey, who wowed audiences with his award-winning role in the Oscar-winning film *American Beauty* (1999), studied at Juilliard before honing his skills on Broadway. In 1986, he made his film debut in Mike Nichols's *Heartburn*, opposite Meryl Streep. A talented stage and screen actor, Spacey was awarded a Tony for his role in *Lost in Yonkers*, and two Academy Awards, for *The Usual Suspects* (1995) and *American Beauty*.

Oprah Winfrey, the popular television personality, debuted in *The Color Purple* (1985), based on the novel by Alice Walker. Cast as Sophia, she brilliantly portrays the travails of a southern African-American woman during the early 1900s. Her impeccable debut performance amazed audiences and critics alike. Nominated for an Academy Award for the role in the Stephen Spielberg film, she was offered countless movie parts, but chose to focus on television, where she continues to be regarded as one of the most influential individuals in the medium's history.

BIBLIOGRAPHY

Adler, Bill. *Fred Astaire: A Wonderful Life.* Santa Barbara, CA: Landmark Books, 1987.

All Movie Guide. March-June, 2001. All Media Guide. <http://www.allmovie.com>

American Movie Classics. March-June, 2001. American Movie Classics. <http://www.amctv.com>

Barnes, Ken. *The Crosby Years.* New York: St. Martin's Press, 1980.

Bauer, Barbara. *Bing Crosby.* New York: Pyramid Publications. 1977.

Bernard, Jami. *First Films.* New York: Citadel Press, 1993.

Billquist, Fritiof. *Garbo: A Biography.* Translated by Maurice Michael.New York: G.P. Putnam's Sons, 1960.

Braun, Eric. *The Elvis Film Encyclopedia.* Woodstock, NY: Overlook Press, 1997.

Carlinsky, Dan. *The Celebrity Yearbook.* Los Angeles: Price/Stern/Sloan, 1983.

Clarke, Gerald. *Get Happy.* New York: Random House, 2000.

Clarkson,Wensley. *Tom Cruise:* Unauthorized. Norwalk, CT: Hastings House,1998.

_____. *Mel Gibson: Living Dangerously.* New York: Thunder's Mouth Press, 1993.

Clinch, Marty. *Harrison Ford: A Biography.* London: New English Library, 1987.

Corliss, Richard. "Queen of the Movies." *Film Comment,* March-April, 1998.

D'Agostino, Annette. *From Soap Stars to Superstars.* Los Angeles: Renaissance Books, 1999.

Dewey, Donald. *James Stewart: A Biography.* Atlanta: Turner Publishing, 1996.

Doctor, Gary L. *The Sinatra Scrapbook.* New York: Citadel Press, 1991.

Dougan, Andy. *Robin Williams.* New York: Thunder's Mouth Press, 1998.

Douglas, Kirk. *The Ragman's Son: An Autobiography.* New York: Simon & Schuster, 1988.

Ebert, Roger. *Roger Ebert's Video Companion,* 1997 Edition. Kansas City: Andrews & McNeel, 1996

Editors of *Who's Who. The Celebrity Who's Who.* New York: World Almanac Books, 1986.

Evans, Peter. *The Mask Behind the Mask: a Life of Peter Sellers.* London: Frewin,1969.

Fornatale, Peter T. and Frank R. Scatoni. *Say Anything: The Movie Quote Game.* New York: Penguin/Putnam, 1999.

Fox-Sheinwold, Patricia. *Too Young To Die.* New York: Bell Publishing Company,1979.

Garceau, Jean with Inez Cook. *Dear Mr. G – The Biography of Clark Gable.* Boston: Little Brown and Co., 1961.

Gardner, David. *Tom Hanks.* London: Blake Publishing, 1999.

Glennon, Lorraine, ed. *The Twentieth Century.* North Dighton, MA: JG Press, 1999.

Harris, Warren G. *Cary Grant: A Touch of Elegance.* Garden City, NY: Doubleday, 1987.

Hill, Anne E. *Denzel Washington.* Philadelphia: Chelsea House Publishers, 1999.

Hirschhorn, Clive. *Gene Kelly.* New York: St. Martin's Press, 1984.

Hotchner, A.E. *Doris Day, Her Own Story.* New York: William Morrow & Company, Inc., 1976.

_____. *Sophia: Living and Loving, Her Own Story.* New York: William Morrow & Company, Inc., 1979.

Hudson, Rock and Sara Davidson. *Rock Hudson: His Story.* New York: William Morrow & Company, Inc., 1986.

Internet Movie Database. January-June, 2001. Internet Movie Database Ltd.<http://www.imdb.com>

Johnstone, Iain. *The Man With No Name: Clint Eastwood.* London: Plexus, 1981.

Joyce, Aileen. *Julia: The Untold Story of America's Pretty Woman.* New York: Windsor Publishing, 1993.

Katz, Ephraim. *The Film Encyclopedia.* 4th ed./rev. by Fred Klein and Ronald Dean Nolen. New York: Harper Resource, 2001.

Knelman, Martin. *Jim Carrey: The Joker is Wild.* New York: Firefly Books, 2000.

Krenz, Carol. *100 Years of Hollywood: A Century of Movie Magic.* New York:Metro Books, 2000.

L., Christophe and Guy Braucort. *Sylvester Stallone.* Paris: Editions PAC, 1985.

Lacey, Robert. *Grace.* New York: G.P. Putnam's Sons, 1994.

Lenburg, Jeff. *Dustin Hoffman, Hollywood's Anti-Hero.* New York: St. Martin's Press, 1983.

Lewis, Jerry with Herb Gluck. *Jerry Lewis, in Person.* New York: Atheneum, 1982.

McCabe, John. *Charlie Chaplin.* Garden City, NY: Doubleday, 1978.

McCann, Graham. *Cary Grant: A Class Apart.* New York: Columbia University Press, 1996.

McGilligan, Patrick. *Jack's Life: A Biography of Jack Nicholson.* New York:Norton, 1994.

Maltin, Leonard, ed. *Leonard Maltin's Movie Encyclopedia.* Spencer Green and Luke Sader, co-eds. New York: Dutton, 1994.

Mast, Gerald. *A Short History of Movies.* New York: Pegasus, 1971.

Maychick, Diana. *Audrey Hepburn, An Intimate Portrait.* Secaucus, NJ: Carol Publishing Group, 1993.

Medved, Harry and Michael Medved. *The Golden Turkey Awards.* New York: G.P. Putnam's Sons, 1980.

Morella, Joe and Edward Z. Epstein. *Brando, the Unauthorized Biography.* New York: Crown Publishers, 1973.

Murphy, Kathleen. "The Good, the Bad and the Ugly: Clint Eastwood as Romantic Hero." *Film Comment,* May-June, 1996.

Oumano, Elena. *Paul Newman.* New York: St. Martin's Press, 1989.

Pfeiffer, Lee. *The John Wayne Scrapbook.* New York: Citadel Press, 1989.

Quinn, Anthony. *One Man Tango.* New York: Harper Collins Publishers, 1995.

Reed, Rex. *From Travolta to Keaton.* New York: William Morrow & Company, Inc., 1979.

Rhode, Eric. *A History of the Cinema From Its Origins to 1970.* New York: Hill and Wang, 1976.

Rollyson, Carl E. *Marilyn Monroe: A Life of the Actress.* New York: DaCapo Press, 1993.

Rooney, Mickey. *Life is Too Short.* New York: Villard Books, 1991.

Schatt, Roy. *James Dean: A Portrait.* New York: G.P. Putnam's Sons, 1982.

Shipman, David. *The Great Movie Stars: The Golden Years.* New York: BonanazaBooks, 1970.

_____. *The Story of Cinema.* New York: St. Martin's Press, 1982.

Sinyard, Neil. *Silent Movies.* New York: Smithmark Publishers, 1995

Slide, Anthony. *The Historical Dictionary of the American Film Industry.* Lanham,MD: Scarecrow Press, 1998.

Spada, James. *The Films of Robert Redford.* Secaucus, NJ.: Citadel Press, 1977.

Spoto, Donald. *Laurence Olivier: A Biography.* New York: Harper Collins Publishers, 1992.

_____. *A Passion For Life: The Biography of Elizabeth Taylor.* New York: Harper Collins Publishers, 1995.

_____. *Rebel: The Life and Legend of James Dean.* New York: Harper Collins Publishers, 1996.

Swindell, Larry. *The Last Hero: A Biography of Gary Cooper.* Garden City, NY: Doubleday, 1980.

_____. *Spencer Tracy.* New York: World Publishing Company, 1969.

Teichman, Howard. *Fonda: My Life.* New York: New American Library, 1981.

Thomas, Bob. "Busier Than Ever, Jack Lemmon Explains Why He Loves His Work." *Associated Press.* April 10, 1998.

Thomas, Tony. *Gregory Peck.* New York: Pyramid Publications, 1977.

Thompson, Charles. *Bob Hope: Portrait of a Superstar.* New York: St. Martin's Press,1981.

Thomson, David. *A Biographical Dictionary of Film.* New York: A.A. Knopf, 1994.

Tornabene, Lyn. *Long Live the King: A Biography of Clark Gable.* New York: G.P. Putnam's Sons, 1976.

Victor, Adam. *The Marilyn Encyclopedia.* Woodstock, NY: Overlook Press, 1999.

Walker, John, ed. *Halliwell's Who's Who in the Movies.* New York: Harper Collins Publishers, 1999.

Wallner, Joan. *Jim Carrey.* Edina, MN: Abdo and Daughters, 1996.

Widener, Don. *Lemmon.* New York: MacMillan Publishing Co., Inc., 1975.

Wills, Garry. *John Wayne's America.* New York: Simon & Schuster, 1997.

Yenne, Bill. *The Field Guide to Elvis Shrines.* Los Angeles: Renaissance Books, 1999.

Yule, Andrew. *Life On The Wire: The Life and Art of Al Pacino.* New York: Donald I. Fine, 1991.

_____. *Sean Connery: From 007 to Hollywood Icon.* New York: Donald I. Fine, 1992.

INDEX